The
Shape of the World

By

Evelyn St. Leger
Author of " Diaries of Three Women of the Last Century "

G. P. Putnam's Sons
New York and London
The Knickerbocker Press
1912

The Knickerbocker Press, New York

To

ROSE HENNIKER-HEATON

WHO WROTE THE WORDS AT THE END OF THIS BOOK

CONTENTS

PART I

THE WORLD

" World—is the great collective idea of all bodies whatever."—*Locke.*

CHAPTER I

THE TOMB OF THE JAVELINS

THE funeral was over. The tenth of his line had been laid to rest in the family vault, which was now declared to be full.

Over the vault was the inscription in Latin, *Ecce homo qui non posuit Deum adjutorem suum*, carved there centuries ago by order of the first Sir Christopher Javelin, who at the end of his days had seen a light shining suddenly in the darkness, which revealed to him the whole reason of his failure in life, but which had been as suddenly extinguished by the hand of death ere he could use that knowledge for purposes of success.

And now another Sir Christopher had been carried through that stone doorway, ninth in direct succession from the Knight of the Javelin; but any illumination ever received from above had long burnt itself out in that once intelligent brain, leaving a stalwart body to live on miserably, long after the death of the mind.

The widow of "the late" walked into the house, turned into a small room on the right, and pulled up the blind. Various members of the family followed, together with the Rector of the parish, the lawyer from London, and the doctor from the neighbouring town.

Soon all the blinds were pulled up all over the house, and voices rose above the proscribed whisper of the last few days. One voice rang with a welcome sound.

"Luncheon is served, my lady."

The sombre guests essayed to tiptoe across the hall with a lamentable want of success that was apparent at every step. Lady Javelin went upstairs and had something brought to her on a tray.

In an hour's time the will was read, but she

was not present. Relations on both sides
came up to her one by one and told her it was
all right: she was to have the place and look
after it till her boy came of age, which was
to be at twenty-five and not twenty-one; and
then invariably they added: "Take my advice,
my dear, and go away for a time while the
house has a thorough, good cleaning. Turn
in the carpenters and the painters and the
paperers, to work their will, and don't
you come back till it is swept and gar-
nished."

Lady Javelin thanked them for what they
said and for their kindness in coming, and
wished them all good-bye.

The doctor came in, breezily rubbing his
hands.

"Fine boy, fine boy, young Chris is a fine
boy! He's done the honours very well. No
flies on him, my lady. He's a son to be
proud of. He means to take you off abroad;
did you know that? You go,"—the doctor
held her hand—"that's my last prescription
for you,"—he bowed before her, a courtly

bow,—"and thank you always for the pleasure it has ever been to be called in by you."

He went down the stairs blowing his nose.

The lawyer followed. He had to catch a train.

"The old will stands. There has been no other. You will manage everything till your son is five and twenty, then the dower house and sixteen hundred a year. Anything I can tell you or do for you—" He smiled the rest of the sentence, and Lady Javelin said:

"Thank you. I know. You have been always more than kind."

"You have made my business here a— pleasure."

He went out and the Rector came in.

"Well," he said.

She looked up. "It is well. I know that. Still I have to make my entry in the book."

The Rector nodded, fiddling with a small key on a chain he held in his hand.

Lady Javelin walked up to a cupboard built into the wall, opened it, and then pressed a spring in the panel of the door. This flew back showing a flat square case standing upright between the outer and inner panels, separated from each other by almost two inches, which space was filled by the book. She took it in both hands and carried it to the table by the fire. Then she sat down.

The Rector fitted the key in the lock, turned back the front of the case, and drew out a red leather volume. It bore the arms and crest of the Javelins emblazoned in gold. The edge was heavily tooled and the paper, rough and discoloured, bore a water-mark that proclaimed it sixteenth century.

The first page was illuminated with the deeds of prowess of the knightly bearer of the name. His birth, his valour, and the manner of his death were set forth in scarlet and blue by

Elizabeth, his wife,

who also wrote these words:

"Hadde i butt knoune bet-er howe tue gide hys steppes hys ende moight have been hap-yer."

This was signed by

Charles Goodenough,

Parish Priest,

1555.

A picture of the tomb was on the next page, beautifully etched, with the Latin inscription standing out clear and distinct. After that a blank, then more illuminations with succeeding owners of the name heading the page, and always thereafter the wife's record was followed by the *Ecce homo qui non posuit Deum adjutorem suum* of the priest-in-charge at the time of the death.

The Rector took a sheet of closely written matter from his pocket, handed it to the widow, and pulled a chair beside hers.

The sound of young feet came up the stairs. The door was burst open without ceremony.

"Come out, Mother!"

The woman let drop the paper. "I can't just now, darling. I must stay and do this."

"Oh! I say!"

Young Sir Christopher curbed his tongue, but spite of this, his fiery eagerness lapped up all the demurs of the room.

"Can't you do it after I 'm gone? I 've got to go to-morrow early, you know, and there 's—there 's a lot for me to see to."

Boyish annoyance at a moment's thwarting, boyish pride in his present position, was apparent in his voice and his looks.

The Rector seemed to feel the influence of his mental attitude for he took the paper, ran his eye through it, and said:

"If you would like me to copy this, the mere facts into the book, while you go out, I can do so and wait to sign the page till you return."

Lady Javelin bent her head in assent. "Thank you very much." Then she smiled, "The living before the dead—don't you agree?" and stood up to go.

"One moment—will you look at what I

have written? It may not be exactly what you would like." The Rector felt it come over him that he was detaining two children instead of one.

Mother and son read the paper together. The boy began to say something as he neared the end, and the woman put her arm round his neck and pressed her hand across his mouth, keeping it there till she had finished, when she released him with a kiss. Then they went downstairs and out by a side door.

The scratching of a quill pen on the paper was for some time the only sound in the house. Suddenly the scratching ceased and a noise began.

Carpenters! unmistakably, both by their voices and their tools.

The quiet man in that quiet room was alert, as if danger threatened. The noise continued and increased. He got up and went to the window. The voices were unrestrained, touched almost with excitement, and the air vibrated with a feverish activity.

He put down his pen and walked to the

door. He roared over the staircase, "What
are you doing down there?" but nobody
answered.

He went down swiftly, following the noise,
till he came upon some men breaking down
a barricaded door.

"Who gave orders for this?"

"Sir Christopher, sir."

"Young Sir Christopher?"

"Sir Christopher, sir."

"Where 's Mr. Dolphin?" (Agent.)

"Outside helping with the windows."

The Rector climbed the stairs. "*Le roi est
mort. Vive le roi.*"

The voices and the clamour downstairs
had ceased before the quill pen was laid aside
and while her ladyship was still absent in the
garden.

The Rector moved restlessly about the
room. He was conscious of a struggle. The
desire to stay where he was till his hostess
returned was warring with a desire to go
downstairs and satisfy a very natural curi-

osity. In small instances of conflict such as this "the Child of Grace" usually gave way to the old Adam. He went downstairs.

All was silent as the grave and, to heighten the effect, a large sheet smelling evilly of carbolic was hung before the doorway where he had seen the men working. He hesitated. Should he lift the sheet and should he go in, or should he only look, just one look? He looked.

A large room with five large windows all flung open wide, and dust lying thick on everything—on the walls, where dimly he could discern the outline of pictures; on the floor, where nothing else could be discerned; on the ceiling, from which a lump of dust greater than any he had ever seen before hung dangerously downwards; on things in the room that gradually shaped themselves into chairs and furniture, made not of wood but of dust.

The Rector stood blinking. Should he go in? Should he? The curtain dropped from his hand, behind him.

So it was for this, for this that a man had wrecked his life's happiness! It was for the guarding of this, an intelligent being had suffered softening of the brain!

A little sound from nowhere recalled him to himself. Fear of discovery made him hot. He felt momentarily more like Adam in the garden than he had ever felt since he had taken orders. He slipped out of the room, and slunk upstairs. He knew he was "slunking," a most uncomfortable proceeding, and his sympathy for the first man in that critical moment of his life was increased to agony point.

Yet he met no one. He heard no one— nothing but the beating of his heart. It was absurd, it was ridiculous he should feel like that. After he had walked about the room for five minutes he began to be sorry he had let his feelings get the better of him. He had done nothing to be ashamed of. By right of a long friendship he was allowed in the house when he pleased and wherever he pleased.

The others came back and joined the Rector looking as if he had not moved.   By-and-by the book was put away.

Lady Javelin had written in the book:

"I did know how to guide his steps, yet his end could not have been more miserable."

The Rector wrote, as other rectors had written, his name and date, below the words, *Ecce homo qui non posuit Deum adjutorem suum.   Psalmorum lii., 8.*

CHAPTER II

SIR CHRISTOPHER

CHRIS took the Rector's arm familiarly as they went downstairs.

"I want you to come and see what I 've done. I hope you 'll approve." He spoke boyishly, standing before the carbolic curtain. "I think my mother has always had a horror of what might be hidden in this room. She has always felt that something unusual occurred here—something more than ordinary to account for the silence and the tragedy of my father's life. When I knew he was dead, I determined to end the mystery before going back to school, that we may face it together."

The boyishness was gone, and there spoke instead a man with all the charm and ring in his voice of a "Young Protector."

The Rector put his hand on his shoulder and pressed it. He could not speak. There seemed nothing to say. There was no mystery. There was only a dusty, dirty room. He knew that, but ought not to have known it.

"My mother would never have the courage to open up the room herself or even give orders for it. She might go on living with an imaginary horror, all unnecessarily. At least, I thought she might, so I took upon myself— I hope you 'll think I did right—to have it opened while I took my mother out of the house. Now I want you to come in with me and see why it was ever closed." He put his hand on the sheet. "There 's nothing to be afraid of. I arranged with Mr. Dolphin that he should stay if there was anything, but there 's nothing. He waved to me on the hill as he went home. Will you come in, and then we will fetch my mother."

They passed inside and stood silent for a moment or two. Chris went up to an object near the table difficult to define. It was a fallen chair. He put out his hand as if to raise it; then stopped. "No, she shall see it just as it is, just exactly as he left it all those years ago. Nothing shall be moved. Wait for us, won't you?"

He was gone, fleeing up those stairs like a normal, happy schoolboy, full of excitement, and presently double steps sounded coming down, and two voices spoke in healthy tones.

"Mother, dear, it's better you should see while I'm here—only there's nothing to see, really nothing; only a little dust and dirt, and that shall be cleared away first thing in the morning, so that we can look at everything before I go. Now!"

Lady Javelin came in and the Rector stood on one side. Three living people in a dead room smelling of carbolic.

The boy held his mother's arm as she picked her way across the dusty floor. She could not speak. The last time she had stood in that room she had been a young and happy woman, the proud and petted wife of the man who had this day been laid to rest in the family vault that was now full.

She stood at the head of the table gazing on the blackened objects that might, when clean, prove to be silver and china and glass.

"There's no cloth," said Chris; "has it moulded away?"

"No, we never used a cloth for dessert."

This was where he had sat the last time—the last time he and she had had a luncheon there together. The table was small and round then, and they had been close to each other, and young. They were very young the last time they had eaten in that room. Chris was a baby upstairs. And ever since then?—Horror! But horror of what and of whose making and why?

She moved round to the wall facing the windows, peering into the square outlines that seemed to denote pictures.

"I 'll clean a corner just for you to see." Chris used his handkerchief as he spoke; then was disgusted at the result.

"Oh, my dear, don't do that! The maids must come in to-morrow, yes, early, as early as you like, but come away now."

She met the Rector's gaze and knew that he too was pondering: "It was for this, for this your happiness was wrecked. Your life was sacrificed for this. He, the man who swore to cherish you, lived a lunatic and died like an animal for this!"

The story was well known. It was no secret throughout the County. There was no secret, and no mystery save in the poor, deluded brain of the master of the house.

That master had married and lived happily after he came into his kingdom for the space of five, little, fleeting years—such happiness as falls to the lot of few to last so long even as that. He and his wife knew it would last for ever. Other people might lose the treasures of life because they were careless or foolish people, but in their case it would not happen. They were different. He said so, and she said so.

When little Chris was four years old his mother went away from home for the first time, because her parents were in trouble and wanted her. She had never visited them

2

alone since her marriage, and the excitement of going was considerably damped by the poignant regret of her spouse at the prospect of losing her for the inside of a week.

She comforted him as best she could, and ordered all his meals for him, and made arrangements with friends that he should dine out three nights during her absence; and when he was still unsatisfied, she then suggested he should have a party of all his old cronies and see which he really liked best, playing the bachelor or playing the married man.

He kissed her in the dining-room after luncheon, holding her to him as though he could never let her go. They heard the carriage come round, but parting, this first parting, was such sweet sorrow they could not end it at the arbitrary command of time. So she nearly lost her train, which started hurriedly and bore her swiftly out of sight, choking but dry-eyed, because she did not want to make it worse for him.

She stayed away nearly a week to her

parents' great joy, mitigated though it was by her oft expressed desire for husband and child. She had a telegram and a letter the first day, two letters the second day, a letter and a post card the third day, a post card without the letter on the fourth day, and nothing on the fifth because it was the day of her return home.

She sat with her head out of the train window from the last station to her own, hoping in some magical way she would thereby see "Him" a bit quicker.

The station was empty, so was the carriage. Nothing but a little message that Sir Christopher was busy and unable to come.

The horses went their usual pace and her heart cried furiously, "Go on! Go on! Oh, do go on!" But the steadiness with which they drove nearly wore her out.

When they reached the house, "He" was not at the door. She walked in and, conscious of domestic eyes, said quietly:

"Is Sir Christopher in?"

"Sir Christopher is in the garden, m'lady."

She laid down her things, looked at her face in the glass, brushing off some imaginary speck, then walked through the hall and out by the garden door.

"Chris! Chris! Oh, darling, where are you?"

She saw him through the trees of the avenue, and called louder. She caught up her skirts and ran. He stood waiting for the onslaught and she flung herself against him.

"Oh, darling, I 've been so frightened. I thought something was the matter. Hug me, Chris, hug me again."

She stood holding his coat, searching his face. "Something is the matter. Chris, what is it? Not baby?"

"Not that I know of. I have n't heard of anything."

"Have n't heard? But have n't you seen him?"

"Well, as a matter of fact, I have n't seen him to-day. I 've been rather, rather busy."

She stood off from him as one would stand

from a stranger whom in mistake one might have accosted familiarly.

"Is anything wrong?"

"I don't know."

"You—don't—know—if anything's wrong? Chris, darling, it is wrong, it must be wrong, if you don't know." She took his hand and held it in both hers: "Tell me what it is."

He took his hand away but he put it through her arm and drew her along with him.

"Don't worry, little woman. It's nothing to do with you. I'm not fit to be left alone, that's all."

"Oh, my angel, you've missed me! That's what the trouble is. I know how you feel. I've been like that all the time. But, Chris, darling, it's all right now. I've come back. Look at me! See! It's all right now!"

She hugged his arm and looked into his face. The tears stood in her eyes, but she didn't care. She knew now what the trouble was and they were tears of relief.

"I see the pram, through the trees. Let us go this way and meet it!"

The nurses stood still and the boy clamoured to be lifted out. He ran bravely along the gravel, then tripped on the grass, and fell.

His mother flew to comfort him, the three joined themselves together, and the nurses went home.

That evening they dined in a little room on the right of the hall. Lady Javelin showed none of the surprise she felt. The changes wrought in her five days' absence were too momentous to speak about save when they two should be alone.

At last, in the library, when the coffee cups had been removed, she sat down on a low stool close to the man she adored. She put her hand on his knee and met with no response. She might have been touching the dead.

A cold, clammy hand seemed to be closing on her heart. She felt frightened of she knew not what, yet feared it was Chris. In some unaccountable way her husband had disappeared; there was something that was like

him sitting in his chair, but it was n't he.
"It was n't he! It was n't Chris!"

The silence in the room, the searching eyes
of the woman, and the averted face of the
man created an uneasy atmosphere, which
both found it difficult to breathe. The tension was broken by a voice speaking very
gently:

"Chris, won't you tell me what it is?"

And the astonishing answer, "What is
what?"

"What is what? What is the matter with
you, with the house, with everything? What
has happened in five, little, tiny days to alter
you from a—a darling—into an old, old man
looking a hundred; what has turned a place
I left full of love and life and laughter into a
miserable mausoleum? Why is the dining-
room shut up? Why are you shut up all inside tight like this, and won't open your
mouth to speak, or your eyes to look at me,
or your arms to let me in? Why, why, Chris,
is this?"

The man shook his head.

"Are n't you going to tell me, dear? I can't help you if you won't."

"I can't."

"Nothing can be as bad as this silence. One is so in the dark. Chris, listen! I don't care what it is, only tell me, let me share it."

Rigid silence.

"Is it, is it something awful? Is it a crime? Have you murdered somebody in that room?"

He gave a short, dry laugh. "No, I have n't done that yet, but I may. You never know when some men will stop, once they begin going downhill."

"My darling, you are not going downhill. I won't let you even if you want to." She put her arms round him. "Listen now to me! You 've got something on your mind and it 's disagreeing with you badly, so badly you think it will disagree with me too if you tell me. Well, it won't, not half so badly as this awful silence. You tell me what it is! You 'll feel ever so much better and then probably we 'll both be able to clear it away, and perhaps laugh about it."

"I don't want you to know."

"No, of course you don't. It 's something horrid, I daresay, but not nearly so horrid as what I shall imagine. I shall think it really is a murder if you don't tell me."

Their positions had changed fundamentally. Before she went away he was her guardian and protector, her prop and stay, her guide, philosopher, and friend. Now he was a sick child, and she was his mother, his nurse, his doctor, his guardian angel, his comforter, his confessor. She was anything and everything he wanted, if he would let her be.

Two o'clock struck. Three o'clock. She was still beside him in the library, wrestling, with tired body, but a brain alert for any chance opening if one should come.

At four o'clock they went upstairs,—the woman heartbroken, and the man acquiescing strangely in the heartbreak.

CHAPTER III

LADY J.

THE next day people came over to see her. She was "not at home" to any one. She only wanted to be with Chris. Though his presence was devoid of pleasure, his absence was a torture.

She must get to the bottom of this mystery. She could not see him a changed man, and she herself remain unchanged.

She could not go into the big dining-room, for the door was locked. She could not ask the servants for the key. She could not let them suppose that she alone in the house was ignorant of its master's doings. For the sake of appearances, she must seem to be acquainted with the reason of the present state of things.

She walked outside, meaning to look in at

the windows; but the windows were still shuttered. Had the servants not been in to open the room? and since when, since when?

She put her hands to her eyes. Was she dreaming a horrible dream, would she wake up presently and find herself still in the train with a nice "'welcome home'" in front of her?

All that day the horrible dream continued. Chris seemed to avoid her company, and when they were together, his appearance was so sad that his wife could not keep the tears from her eyes.

A note was brought to her late in the day requiring an answer:

DEAR LADY JAVELIN,

Will you see me? I want to tell you how sorry I am about Tuesday night's affair. My husband is ashamed to come himself until he knows you will forgive him.

Ever sincerely yours,
MONA CUMBERLAND.

This was like so much Greek to Lady Javelin. She read it through twice with the intention of refusing the request. Then it dawned on her that the meaning of the mystery was contained in the note. She said to the servant, "Who brought this?"

"Her ladyship was in the carriage, but has driven on to the village, and will call back for an answer in a few minutes."

"I will see her ladyship, but no one else."

The next impulse was to tell Chris, to go to him, to show him the note, to ask his opinion of it, to "wonder" over it together, and to laugh at the idea of Lord Cumberland's wanting her forgiveness; but this natural impulse had to be suppressed. Chris must n't be worried; she must manage things alone now; she could tell him afterwards—if—if it were wise to tell him. Thus did the new-born nurse in her rise on behalf of the patient in him.

The two women met, somewhat tentatively. Each was puzzled by the other. Lady Javelin was quietly receptive; her guest was rapidly explanatory. Within a short time they were laughing, both of them. The tension had vanished from the visit, due to the good sense of the hostess. If it was possible to laugh at the situation, she was ready enough to laugh. She was almost ready for hysterics when complete knowledge took the place of complete ignorance. The relief was so intense, the rebound nearly lost her her balance.

When they parted, they kissed each other from an overflow of gratitude on either side. Their lords were a disgrace, but then—these men!—one must forgive them when they are penitent, and his lordship of Cumberland was very, very penitent. He would come himself the next day to be properly forgiven.

The gong rang as the hall door closed. Lady Javelin flew up the stairs like a girl. Her eyes were bright and shining; her face was flushed a brilliant pink. She dressed in a few minutes and was down, holding out a hand to her husband as they walked into the little room for dinner. She talked all through the meal, told him gaily of her doings when away, related the plot of a new book to fill up time, caught his eye and smiled at him whenever he would permit such a liberty, and refused, absolutely, to share the despondent gloom of her spouse.

That night when he went to bed he found her sitting up reading on her sofa. He went and sat down beside her more from habit than because he had anything to say. She put an arm round his neck and kissed him. "Cheer up darling, I know all about it. You 've been very, very naughty, all of you. It was n't your fault; it was the others, I 'm sure of that. But they are all so sorry we won't say any more about it, will we?"

She felt him stiffen as she spoke, but she held him tighter. "I shall have the room opened to-morrow early, if you will let me have the key, and when the mess is all cleared up, we 'll forget it ever happened and things can be just as sweet and nice as they 've always been."

She kissed the tip of his ear which was next her.

"Say you 're glad I know without your having to tell me. It 's thanks to Lady Cumberland. She brought messages from most of your party. They 've all been as miserable as you have; but it 's all right now, is n't it, Chris? We 'll clear it all up to-morrow and never think of it again."

The woman's optimism was in sharp contrast to the moodiness of the man.

"It can never be the same again."

"Oh, yes it can, dear. You give me the key now, and to-morrow you go for a long ride, and stay out all day and when you come back, you 'll find everything perfectly right, and then you 'll give me a hug to make up for the two days I have n't had a hug at all."

It was the mother talking now with a dear but somewhat refractory child. But the child refused to give up the key that night at its mother's bidding,—"She could have it in the morning." And with wisdom new-born from on high, Lady Javelin refrained from pressing the point but took the refractory child to her heart, gaining comfort for herself because she thought she was comforting him.

Now is it conceivable that when the morning came, the husband of this lady, the master of the house, the tenth baronet of his line, in whose hands lay the happiness of his home and those belonging to him, reviewing the conversation of the night before, saw in it only an effort of the inferior sex to deal cunningly with a member of the superior sex, and that member, HIMSELF? It is quite inconceivable under the circumstances, yet it is a fact. Here was a man, a highly educated man, of average intelligence, regarded as an example in the neighbourhood, the father of a family, a large employer of labour; here he was, not only incapable of himself correcting a mistake of his own making, but positively capable of hindering the woman who loved him from wiping out his misdeeds with common soap and water, not to mention sense.

"I 'll think about it," he said, with his silly head up in the air, when starting out for his ride, "I 'm not sure it 's good for you to have your own way in everything. I 'll see when I come home whether I 'll have that room opened or not," and he left her gaping after him as one would gape at the devil if he assumed the disguise of one's nearest and dearest with intent to take one in.

All the exquisite motherly feeling that had welled over and covered every defect now suddenly dried up. The woman of many parts,—the mother, the nurse, the doctor, the angel,—seemed to be slipping out of existence. What was left of her stood vacantly staring after the departing figure. The bottom seemed to have fallen out of the world.

And as she stood there, lost in wonderment and misery, Mr. Dolphin, the agent, appeared at her side.

"Good morning," he said, taking off his hat, and waited.

"Good morning," she answered and made a resolution. "Come with me into the house." He turned and followed her to the business room.

"Mr. Dolphin, why is the dining-room locked up?"

Yesterday she would have cut out her

3

tongue rather than ask that question of
any one.

"Sir Christopher locked it, I understand,
on Tuesday night."

"Yes, but it can't stay locked, Mr. Dolphin."

"Sir Christopher has the key with him."

"Yes. We must open it without the key.
I shall be glad if you will have it done at once.
I want the room cleaned out, and all the
silver and things put away."

Mr. Dolphin's jaw dropped, and the lady
speaking to him hardly knew the voice to be
hers.   It was astonishing she should be giving
an order on her own account, and an order
possibly contrary to her husband's wishes.

They stood facing each other.

"I 'm sorry, but Sir Christopher told me
that room was to remain closed for the
present."

Her ladyship pulled her senses together.
"The room is dirty. I can't live with a dirty
room in the house."

"No. I 'm at a loss to understand why it
was not set in order before your return."

"Of course, Mr. Dolphin, you must break in that door, or pick the lock, or something. I want everything tidied up before Sir Christopher's return."

A servant interrupted them. "Lord Cumberland in the library, m' lady."

She turned away.

"Please have it done at once." Then she walked across the hall and opened a door on the other side.

Her visitor in riding breeches stood on the hearth-rug, surveying the toes of his boots. He came up to her and took her hand, not letting it go, but holding it in a nervous grip, scanning her face.

"Lady J., I don't know what to say. I hear you 've taken it like an angel." He still held her hand while she walked to a sofa, whereon they both sat down. "We 're most awfully sorry about it. I 'm only a forerunner, the rest are all coming to pay you their respects. You don't know what we felt the next day. 'Pon my word, I was so ashamed of myself, I told my lady I—well—

there 's nothing for it, but to own up and say we are sorry, and hope that you 'll forgive us. Will you? I 'm most awfully sorry, Lady J., really you know I am."

He kept his eyes on his boots all the time he spoke, and his voice and manner both betokened sincerity. He was a big man, Lady J. had always liked him, at the present moment she thought him adorable.

"It is very nice of you to come and say this," she said. "Of course I forgive you, but——"

He glanced up anxiously, "and the others, Chris and the whole lot?"

"Of course, but——" His face was a study, so earnest and solemn, and the situation was so extremely comical, she began to laugh. He looked surprised and polite, she tried to stop, feeling mirth to be perhaps out of place, and in trying to stop, she laughed more, calling herself names for doing so, and yet unable to cease.

"It 's awfully jolly of you taking it like this. I wish I knew what you are laughing at."

"It 's very silly of me, but—you see I don't know what it is I 've got to forgive. I don't really know what any of you did!"

The "did" was on a top note, faint but shrill.

"Ripping!" His laugh rivalled hers. He roared, throwing his head back in the cushions and howling with his mouth wide open.

How they laughed! The relief was intense and boundless. She felt quite weak before they stopped, it sounded so like a duet, the bass and the treble mixed.

"Well now, do tell me Lord Cumberland, what exactly was the wickedness?"

"Er—well er—may I smoke? You see, you were away," he struck a match, and she nodded assent, "and Chris asked us all to dine and cheer him up!—Charley Crooks and Tim Popples and myself and young Larkin and George Maydew and all the old lot—and we agreed to have some fun. Well old Chris did us proud. He got out his best champagne —poison to most of us you know. Still we could n't refuse. And then some '64 port, not to mention old brandy of the very finest. And we got talking about the good old times, and the old four bottle men, and—well you know I 'm very abstemious as a rule, drink barley water for lunch often—and 'pon my soul, Lady J., I don't believe any of us know exactly what did happen, but not to put too fine a point on it, I think

'We all got drunk and had a jolly spree.'

"I know it was disgraceful.   I 'm not trying to excuse us, but you were away, you know, and there we were, singing, Lord how we sang! and gassing away, one good story on top of another, and then we tried to break up—I do hope you won't be shocked—but not one of us could find the bell.   We had a regular steeple-chase after it all round the room, and when we could n't find it, we started looking for the door, and we—well we were n't any more successful at that—and—well it does seem awful —but you know, we think the servants found us in the morning, and, Lady J., I can't tell you what beasts we felt when we thought of you."

Lady Javelin was quite sober now. "It was rather horrid, was n't it? But I 'm glad you 've told me; I would rather know the worst."

"They 've had a pretty bad time since with the wives. Madam Maydew cut up fearfully rough and talked of a legal separation and the Lord knows what. Poor old George is like a dog with his tail between his legs. Some of them say they would never forgive such a thing, and they don't know but what you 'll cut the lot of us and end all the happy times we 've had here."

Lady J. shook her head. "Please tell them I understand how it happened. I 'm glad every one is sorry; it is a proof that we 've advanced since our grandfather's days, is n't it? They would have done this sort of thing every night of their lives and nobody would ever have apologised to the lady of the house, would they?"

"I suppose not; it seems impossible. We did feel—well jolly ashamed. Times change and so does public opinion." He got up and

held out his hand. "Good-bye, Lady J., I go
away with a debt of gratitude I can never
hope to pay."

The visitor departed and his hostess returned
to the door on the opposite side of the hall.
She tried the handle, the lock still held.   Mr.
Dolphin had failed to do her bidding.   While
standing there she heard his voice speaking
to some one, a carpenter no doubt, or a lock-
smith.   A little patience and the room could
still be cleared before Chris's return.

She heard the other voice answer Mr.
Dolphin, and it made her feel queer.   It was
her husband's.   Both men were arguing and
coming in her direction.   She felt a sensation
of fear come over her—she knew not why.
There could be nothing to fear, yet she was
afraid; and in her very desire to be elsewhere,
her feet seemed suddenly glued to the floor.

"I'm so glad you've come back, dear,"
she said, conscious of the nervousness in her
voice.   "I do so want to have this room cleaned
out."

Chris looked at her, and as he looked,

something she had never seen before rose
into his face and made it evil, malignant,
vindictive.

"I've just been telling Dolphin I won't
have it opened, so you need n't worry about
it. I don't intend to use that room again.
I 've my own reasons for it, and I wish them
to be attended to."

The sensation of fear was justified. She
had been married to this man for five years,
infinitely happy with him, and he stood before
her now as a complete stranger, worse, as a
stranger she would never willingly entertain
for five minutes; and he came in the stolen
guise of her darling Chris.

She gave a little cry. She could n't strangle
it, and she did n't care who heard. Mr.
Dolphin must see, every one must see that
something awful had happened, something
quite awful to Chris.

The three remained motionless for a moment;
then the master of the house walked off to his
den. The agent wished he could drop through
the ground. The lady put out her hand as if

in need of support.   He stepped towards her
and crooked his arm deferentially.

"Can I?   May I?"

But he did n't say any more.   She clutched
his coat where it wrinkled in the bend of his
elbow and held it tight.   Something bright
splashed on to the stone paving of the hall.

Poor little lady of a grand old name!   Poor
little broken mistress of a grand old house!

CHAPTER IV

THE OTHERS

A GROUP of men met at the park gates soon after three o'clock that afternoon. They were Charley Crooks, Tim Popples, young Sir Guy Larkin, and George Maydew. They all agreed to walk to the house on foot. They represented the married element in Tuesday night's party and were coming at the bidding of their wives, plus their own consciences, to pay their respects to the very popular wife of their naughty and popular host.

"Come on, Larkey! You 've got to do the talking and we' ll act chorus. Anything you say we 'll agree to. Only don't be too discursive. Just say we wish she'd been at home; then all would have been well, See, old man?

Wish we could meet her! 't would be easier outside than in. Sh—there she is. Larkey, there she is!"

A slim figure in white came out of the garden door and turned abruptly to the left. The men, conscious that she had n't seen them, stepped up briskly and overtook her by the cedar tree, under which were some chairs.

"Lady J.!" Sir Guy cleared his throat, "Lady J.!"

The slim figure stood still, and when the four men saw the face, they felt turned to stone.

"I 'm not at—Oh!—Sir Guy—I did not see who it was."

She held out a hand to him and bowed to the others. They knew themselves to be images now, incapable of anything good or bad, whereas they had lately been apostrophising themselves as dogs—occasionally rather gay dogs.

Sir Guy bending over the hand he held murmured gently. "Will you speak to us? We don't deserve it, but will you?"

The parasol wavered over his head. Her
ladyship looked at his bowed figure and the
other three standing back bareheaded. As
she looked, she forgot about the horrible old
dining-room and only thought they were
dears.

"Yes. Come and talk to me, will you? I
did not mean to see anybody to-day. I 've—
got rather a headache. There must be thun-
der about."

The pink rims to her eyes and the purple
shadows had to be accounted for somehow.

"Oh! have you, Lady J.? I 'm so sorry,"
sprang automatically from four manly throats.
The wooden images assumed movements
most lifelike in arranging chairs and cushions
and a foot-rest close together under the cedar
tree.

One man pulled out his cigarette case. Sir
Guy Larkin frowned at him, a frown which
plainly said, "Put that away, sir," and the
man slipped it back into his pocket.

The three sat down awkwardly. The chosen
spokesman laid his hat on the grass and then

suddenly knelt on both knees in front of Lady Javelin. He folded his arms and quite gravely said:

"We, your humble but devoted servants, beg to express our sincere regret for the abominable mess we made of your house in your absence the other night, and to hope that our present deep sorrow and future good conduct will prove to you that we are not altogether unworthy of your forgiveness, should you some day condescend to give it us."

"Dear Sir Guy, get up. Of course you're forgiven, all of you. It's too nice of you to come and see me. Her eyes fell on each in turn. I'm sorry it happened, because I know it's made you all miserable, but such delightful penitents should not have to wait a moment for absolution."

"Are we absolved?" Sir Guy was still on his knees, his arms tightly folded.

"Not only absolved. You never did it!"

"Lady J., you're a brick!" He bent and kissed her hand where it lay on her gown. Then he stood up.

"Lady J., you 're a brick!" was repeated three times over by the adoring penitents. "I say, but you are a brick, you know. My wife said you would n't forgive us! Can you really forgive us? We must have made an awful mess. I suppose it was all jolly well cleared away before you saw it?"

Sir Guy said, "Righto! Not another word boys. The incident never took place! But her ladyship advises you by me that you don't do it again. Now you may smoke."

Larkin turned to his hostess: "Is that so, have we your permission or will it make your head worse?"

"You 've taken it away. I forgot I had one," she laughed.

"What a blessed memory you have for frail and foolish man!" He looked as if he would like to kiss her. Instead he lit a cigarette.

The master of the house came out later, when tea appeared. He found two men playing croquet, one talking to his wife, one throwing a ball for his small son. He had always been regarded as an addition to the gaiety of the moment anywhere, and he was hailed genially with "Hullo, Chris!"

His response to their warm reception can only be described as tepid. He nodded truly, but it was a nod of duty not of pleasure. The greatest optimist amongst them could not feel that their host was glad to see them. They tried in the new purity of their souls to chaff him about Tuesday night. Their own speedy absolution gave them some idea of what rapturous comfort must have been his after he 'd got through the *mauvais quart d'heure*, badly deserved by the poor old chap.

But Chris was n't "taking any" as the saying is; the chaff fell flat; and sweet Lady J. looked as if her headache had come back. So the party broke up, and Chris and his wife and child, followed by a lot of dogs, walked with the men to the gate.

"Good-bye; no not good-bye, Lady J., I cannot bear it. Woe is me, say not good-bye."

"Then au revoir."

"That 's better. Au revoir."

"Auf Wiedersehen."

"Better still Auf Wiedersehen!"

"À dieu, Sir Guy."

"The best of all." He waved his handkerchief foreign fashion—"à dieu, à dieu, Miladi and Milord, à dieu, à dieu."

The others turned again, raising their hats.

"So long, Lady J., so long!"

Round the bend of the road in silence, out of sight, but not out of mind.

"What's up, Larkey, what's up?"

But Larkey shook his head and growled.

"Did you look at the dining-room windows?"

"Of course."

"Did you see?"

"I'm not blind."

"Good Lord, what fools we were! Sorry if we upset their matrimonial comfort."

Larkey wasn't going to be drawn, and they returned to their separate homes without speaking.

Husband and wife played with the boy till he went to bed; then the woman, trying to

4

speak lightly, as if the subject were of no moment to either of them, told the man why the visitors had called that afternoon. She said it was nice of them to come, and still nicer the way they offered their *amende honorable.* She said it made it so easy to forgive anything in the world, when people were sorry like that.

The man broke through his sulkiness for the moment. "H'm! I 'm taking it all in. Cut at me, I suppose, because I 'm not sorry exactly like everybody else."

His wife slipped her hand into his, at least as much of hers as his would admit.

"Darling, you 're much sorrier. I know that it 's because you—care more, but if you could, if you only could, say it, and throw your arms round me as they did, you 'd feel——"

"WHAT?"

"O Chris, don't shout at me like that. It hurts my head."

"Who threw his arms round you?"

"Nobody, dear, don't be silly."

"You said so! Am I not to believe what you say?"

"Yes, of course, in a sensible fashion. If you 'd only be sensible, Chris, as you used to be, it would make things much easier for me."

"I did n't know your life was so hard!"

"It never has been before. It won't be now if you 'll, if you 'll kiss me and open the dining-room door."

The man's face might have softened at the reasonable request. He might have gathered her to his heart. He might have whispered in her ear, "Sorry darling, I 'm sorry to have been such a pig. We 'll go and open that horrible door together, and I 'll show you the worst there is, and you shall work your own sweet will in the room, and I 'll pay little woman for the mischief done. I 'll pay up, Sweetheart, like a man."

But he did not say that. His face hardened instead, and represented no doubt the flint-like consistency of his heart, for he did not hesitate to deny her the request of her lips.

Alas and alack for the absence of that old-

fashioned something we used to hear about
long ago, so old-fashioned, so out of date, we
never talk about it now Yet it was something that Charley Crooks, and Tim Popples,
and Lord Cumberland, and Guy Larkin,
and poor George Maydew had, and Christopher had not. Was it "The Grace of God,"
do you think?

CHAPTER V

AN ATTEMPT

AND this small matter in the great affairs
of life, this trifling incident of Sir Christopher Javelin keeping his dining-room locked,
this petty domestic annoyance, fast assumed
an interest out of all proportion to public
advantage. Even as a little spot on the finger
can inflame and spread till the whole hand
suffers from an apparently small but rankling
sore, so does a community suffer if one of its
members acts in such a way that his continued
action provokes a state of resentment or
irritation set at large.

Sir Christopher had done no more than the
men of his set. His offence had been their
offence, but his integrity had been a good
deal less. He had failed to comply with the

universal law. He had made a mistake, and instead of vigorously correcting it by wiping it out of existence, he chose to devise a miser-able system whereby he could support the original error and its ill-begotten brood.

As the days went on, the story of that Tuesday's folly grew until it became a scandal in the neighbourhood. When it was known, with the rapidity that such things always are known, that Lady Javelin had shown no signs of temper, but had merely asked that a dirty room might be cleaned without delay and had been refused, the thing of course became a crying scandal, and what had first been laughed at as a foolish frolic on the part of men who ought to have known better now provoked a good deal of head-shaking over a distasteful subject affecting the honour of the county.

The only question in the mind of the hearers of the escapade had been, "What will Lady Javelin say when she comes home?" Will she forgive her husband and condemn his guests? Will she make a terrible row and say disagree-

able things about man in general and certain
women's husbands in particular? Will she
eventually forgive the other men because of
their unoffending wives, and will she vent a
most natural annoyance on the man who
permitted such a disgraceful orgy in his own
house?

There were no surmises as to Sir Christopher's conduct. There was only one thing he
could do: that was to have all traces of the
revel removed without delay, then, to meet
his lady, hat in hand, and essay to disarm her
criticism of his former procedure by the un-
doubted charm of his present bearing. All
those who knew Sir Christopher knew this
was what he would do. What they did not
know, and what gave life and vigour to the
situation, was what Lady Javelin would do.

Consequently, when the true facts leaked
out of what they had both done, all the men
condemned Sir Christopher and all the women
praised his wife. The other men had it well
rubbed in what their fate would have been,
had any of them acted host on such an occa-

sion with similar ill-timed results; and an affair that could have been dismissed with a laughing grace to oblivion, now became the absorbing topic of conversation.

When Lord and Lady Cumberland heard the general version of the tale going round, they politely declined to believe it. They said they knew the Javelins both so well, were so acquainted with their characters, were so thoroughly aware of their devotion to each other, that it was impossible to hold such an idea as Sir Christopher's refusing any reasonable request of his wife.

However, to prove assurance doubly sure, they sent out invitations to dinner that the Javelins themselves might by their mere presence and behaviour give the lie direct. From the Cumberlands' point of view this dinner was not the success they hoped it would be.

Lady J. played up well, but her gaiety was forced, out of compliment to her friends, and was not the natural gaiety to which they were used. Sir Christopher was silent with the

gloomy silence that makes ordinary and
polite conversation appear an intrusion, and
when they left, it was a relief, yet a relief
combined with a sense of failure.

After that the situation became acute. Was
it possible that one man's pig-headedness
was to act as a spoil-sport on the whole County?
It was not possible. In a hospitable shire
such as this, where the large landowners lived
on their land, where the lords and the commons
mixed and mingled on equal terms a dozen
times in a week, where each great house did
its fair share in the entertainment of its neighbours, with such traditions, such surroundings,
and under such circumstances, it was not
possible to permit the continuance of a closed
door by the order of one against the decree
of the many.

It was generally agreed amongst the men
that the soft persuasions of his wife having
failed to bring him to his senses, Sir Christopher
must now be made to yield by the combined
forces of the male population who numbered
him as their friend. They told Lady J. they

intended to rescue her from the dungeon of despair in which she had been cast by a mistake in judgment. They rather prided themselves on the part they meant to play. It had a glorifying effect on them to pose as chivalrous knights to a lady and her child, for they never forgot that little Chris had to be considered. If his own father set him aside, it behooved them all the more to act as sponsors for the present well-being and future happiness of the next man in.

Lady J. was grateful, in a manner that misery almost disguised. For how could she bear, how could any woman bear, to feel that outside help was necessary in a conflict of wills between two who for years had lived in unexampled intimacy and devotion?

Therefore she decided to fight to the finish this fight that daily she knew to be of the devil. Single handed she would fight—and yet not single handed, for surely on her side there would be God.

She told no one what she meant to do, but a month from her return home, a whole month

of distress, of torture, of patience, of love,
bruised and battered, but still love, bright
and shining that day month, or rather late
that night, saw her come out from her bed-
room in a short petticoat with her gown pinned
up round her waist, a large apron, and a cap
or white thing covering over her hair.

She went to the housemaid's cupboard and
collected a pail, some flannel, some soap, and
an armful of brushes and brooms. These she
carried through the quiet house and placed
outside that door, the voluntary opening
of which she believed would break an evil
spell.

The physical exertion brought a healthy
colour to her cheeks. She turned towards
Sir Christopher's den, paused with her hand
on the banister rail, looking up at the moon
shining through the hall window, then bowing
her head, knelt suddenly and almost momentarily on the bottom stair.

A cry for help? scarcely. More an act of
reverence to the Lord of Battles who would
crown her efforts with success.

She opened Sir Christopher's door and walked up to him where he was half dozing in a chair.

"Wake up," she said, "I want you to help me."

He gazed at her with the stolid gaze she had endured for the last month. "I want you to help me" might surely have stirred him rather than the more natural phrase, "I have come to help you." This latter a man might conceivably resent; the former he could not.

"Wake up, Chris dear, wake up!" She held out her hand and the man put his into it, instinctively, because it had been a habit of years.

She held it silently, conscious of the forces working for his salvation. "Come," she said gently, "come with me, I want you."

"What for?" suspiciously alert.

"You know what it is for. You and I are going to clear up that room, so that nobody else shall see what it is like. I 've got everything ready, but its——"

The man frowned, "What 's that in your hand?"

She did not know she had anything in her hand. Looking down she saw an unfamiliar scrubbing-brush in her grasp, and laughed.

"This is the thing we 've got to use. I don't think I 'm much good at it, but perhaps you can manage the difficult bits. It will be great fun. Only we must not make a noise and wake the house."

She tiptoed softly to the door as she spoke. Chris followed her as if absently, his hands deep in his pockets. When he saw her stooping over the pail, he seemed to recognise her motive in calling him.

"Now," she said, picking up the soap gingerly in the flannel, "you carry in the water and I 'll——"

Her sentence tailed away into silence, for the invisible forces of which she was conscious suddenly met and crashed with an opposing force of apparently equal strength. The whole man changed as she looked at him. From being half awake and wholly indifferent, he stepped ready armed on to the line of defence, facing her, metaphorically speaking, sword in hand.

She did not feel afraid. She was not fighting Chris. Chris had disappeared. In his place was the devil.

She did not lose her head with the shock. She knew instinctively that diplomacy was all the more necessary. Diplomacy had never been necessary in her dealings with her husband. What she had wished, he had wished. They had been two people of one mind; now, it was different.

"Will you help me?" she said again by way of conciliating his satanic majesty, ignoring the little rule of etiquette that forbids Beelzebub casting out Beelzebub from places where he has a strong motive for remaining.

In the present instance the man took up his position back to the door the woman wished to open, facing her in an attitude of determined opposition. She felt all the time she was parleying with the devil, yet she said, "Now, dear," as though she were talking with her husband.

"I 'm not—going—to open this room, not if you keep me standing on guard all night."

"No? then let me open it. We can't keep it locked for ever, you know. The Hobsons and Fitz-Jameses are coming to stay next week."

"Are they?"

"You know they are, and there 's no need for them to find us all at sixes and sevens."

"You are simply wasting your breath talking like this. I intend to keep this room closed or any room in the house closed that I have a fancy to. It 's my house; you are my wife; you 'll oblige me by seeing my wishes are attended to."

"Chris, if you don't do this thing—to please me, because I ask it, I 'll never so long as I live ask anything else of you, never."

"All right! So be it!"

"So be it! Now I know who you are. You 're the devil!"

"Thank you. You are very complimentary."

Her flash of perception was speedily dimmed by previous knowledge. Within two minutes she was using all the wiles known to woman —in vain. She reasoned with him. She spoke softly. She told him she loved him. She prayed him not to be hard-hearted against her. She went down on her knees, forgetting he was the devil and thinking only he was her husband. Down on her knees, holding his hand, she tried with all her strength to break the spell that was on him, and failed.

She weighted the scale with his love for her, for his son, for his mother. She threw in his pride of the name and the place. She flung pell-mell on one another all the tender memories of years, and they weighed nothing in the balance against her. In the other scale was a stubborn will and a heart of stone.

She rose. "Never again Chris. I'll never ask you again—anything, never."

"So you said before, and as I remarked then, I remark now: 'All right! So be it!'"

She almost saw red streaks of light shooting from him. She almost smelt something sulphurous. She felt stung with darts thrown at her, and threw back in response what was handiest—soap, flannel, a broom, brushes— one after the other. She kicked the pail and rejoiced to see it hit his shins and the water run into a pool.

As always, things rejected intended for help, turned to his hurt. And the devil who had done away with her husband and had thought to deceive her by taking his place, laughed at her. Laughed at her! Mocked her in her misery, as she ran from his presence maddened with rage and grief.

5

CHAPTER VI

AND A FAILURE

AFTER this, feeling ran very high in the County.   Lady Javelin's illness provoked many comments not altogether to the credit of Sir Christopher.   She was very very ill.

The doctors were at their wits' end to know the cause.   They turned to the master of the house for light and information.   All they got from him was a surprising description of Lady Javelin's extraordinary behaviour the night of the thirteenth: how she had suddenly come to him at midnight, dressed up like a servant, and had proceeded to throw household utensils at his head; how these very things had been found scattered about the floor the next morning; how the carpet was irretrievably spoilt by water upset in the scrimmage; and how his shin still bore the mark of the bucket or pail which his wife, in a temper, had kicked at him.

A most unseemly performance! But accountable? Could Sir Christopher account for the outburst in any way? Had her ladyship shown signs previously of any lack of self-control?

Sir Christopher could not say she had. He had always hitherto regarded his wife as a level-headed woman, most amenable to his wishes. No, he had never experienced any trouble with her before.

But was this sudden outburst wholly unreasonable, or could he search his mind or memory for some foundation, however flimsy it might appear to him?

Sir Christopher admitted somewhat reluctantly that like all women Lady Javelin was an adept at getting her own way. He had let her have her head for years. He was very fond of her and he had seldom denied her anything. However, when he put his foot down, he in-

tended to keep it down, and lately he had issued an order which he was sorry to say had given great offence to his wife, who had used all her powers of persuasion to induce him to rescind that order, but which he had declined to do. It was no doubt her failure to move him which induced this regrettable show of temper.

The doctors bowed towards him. Possible, it was quite possible. But did the order,— Sir Christopher would pardon their seeming curiosity—did the order affect Lady Javelin personally, could it affect her physically or mentally?

Sir Christopher allowed himself to smile condescendingly. "Socially," he said, "it could only affect her socially. I decided to close the large dining-room in the house and use the small breakfast room. I had my own reasons for doing so, and these her ladyship knew."

So much for Sir Christopher. So little for the doctors. They nodded wisely and left foolishly.

In after years one of these men was called

in again and saw the same two people with the situation reversed.   He then perplexed his younger colleague on the journey back to town by quoting more than once.

> "The dog went mad and bit the man,
> The dog it was that died."

He felt it was n't quite correct in the context and showed signs of worry, but this is by the way.

Sir Christopher's plausible account, if good enough for outsiders, failed to win the approval of those chivalrous spirits inside the pale who had sworn to restore happiness to the Lady J. of their hearts. They descended on her husband in ones and twos and in crowds. Separately and collectively, they argued with him, reasoned with him, rated him, and finally abused him in language that was strong and vigorous if somewhat out of date as belonging to a rude and rougher age.

All to no purpose.   Sir Christopher merely turned nasty and intimated his intention to rule according to his own will, in his own house. If his friends did not like his rule, the remedy was simple.

Lord Cumberland said, "Come, come, Chris, you are n't surely going to quarrel with us over such a foolish affair. Where 's the pleasure for you in having your own way if it 's going to upset your wife and everybody else? It is n't worth it, man. Besides we all feel more or less guilty in the matter. It is n't fair to any of us and it is n't cricket. 'T is n't cricket."

Failure attended these efforts, and anger took possession of the souls whose bodies in the first instance had been partially to blame. The men one and all were furious. They understood now how Lady Javelin had thrown things. They felt like throwing things themselves. Such pig-headed obstinacy deserved to be attacked with a poker, since the gimlet of commonsense was obviously futile.

When a collection of individuals feel strongly, they usually act together in a manner that

each one separately might possibly condemn.
They did so in this instance.

They raided Javelin Hall one night after
dark with every imaginable tool for breaking
down walls and doors that the hearts of a
cheery and earnest-minded crew could devise.
They set to work on the outside of that closed
room, and having opened a bolted window
and smashed in a shutter, they were proceeding by gentler methods to force an entry when
their former friend and host appeared before
them.

He was standing in the middle of the floor
of the room they had raided, the door was
open behind him, and the red light from the
hall shone in on him where he stood. He had
on an old hunt dress coat, and something dark
and snaky moved silently over the floor beside
him.

His face was white, even his lips. His eyes
were flashing fire. The colour from the lamp,
the colour of his coat, the coiling thing beside
him all gave but one impression. Every man
simultaneously said, "The Devil!"

Then swish and full came an onslaught
that sent them backwards.   Helter-skelter,
tumbling over one another, they hurried side-
ways from the house they had recently braved
with a frontal attack.

The snakelike thing in Sir Christopher's
hand reared its brazen nozzle and flung its
spume far out into the night, and the white
grinning face with its scarlet surroundings,
enframed in the broken window, made an
impression that the chivalrous souls were not
very likely to forget.   Running with undignified haste from a fire-hose did not appear
funny to any of them at the moment, though
it made a good story afterwards when the
bitterness of defeat was passed.

Thus all was done that could be done to
free a man from bondage.   That he had ever
got there was more or less accidentally his
own doing.   That he persisted in remaining
bound was also his own doing of set and
stubborn purpose.

When Lady Javelin recovered her strength
she went away for a time with little Chris,—

a time for recovering her energies, for resetting her judgment, for re-sorting her ideas, for rearranging her world.

As she journeyed home again, there hovered within her the faintest fluttering hope that a miracle might have taken place in her absence, a miracle to set right this time what some black magic had sent wrong last time. It would n't be a greater miracle to find Christopher, her darling Christopher, alive now, than it had been to find him dead then.

Dead! If his body had been dead, it would have been terrible, terrible; but it could not have been the agony of that other find, the death of the spirit, the spirit which giveth life.

"Dear God, could n't a miracle happen?"

She reached home, but there was no welcome for her, save from the unrestrained barks of the dogs, and from old servants in deferential restraint.

Sir Christopher did not come in till dinner time. Then, standing in the doorway, he said, "I hope you 're better, I won't come near you.   I 'm rather muddy," and disappeared till the second gong.

After dinner he had some papers to read and went to his den alone.   Every action, every look, every grudging word, betokened his deep displeasure at her return, or was it her existence?

She sat on alone till past ten o'clock, then pushed open his door, and said quietly, "I 'm going upstairs, Chris, now."

"Are you?"   He turned round in his chair. "Then good-night.   I 've changed my room, you 'll find.   I 'm sleeping downstairs.   It suits me better and I beg in future I may not be troubled with any more midnight visits. One such is enough to last me a life time.   As you have so little regard for my wishes, I have taken precautions which will, I think, make it almost impossible for even you to go against them.   Good-night."   He turned back in his chair, and she closed the door.

The next day she saw him at breakfast when he read his letters silently, putting each one into his pocket in a strange, furtive sort of manner. He seemed to eat a great deal, she thought, omitted to help her to anything, and left without having spoken a word. She saw him in the hall later and asked if he would be in to lunch. He said "No, nor to dinner either." He would not be back till late but nothing need be kept for him.

She stood motionless for a few minutes, then turned round the corner by the closed door. It was barred, with five iron bars driven at either end into the stone wall. She came back, crossed the hall, and went out by the garden entrance. A little way down the gravel walk she stopped, looking at the big windows of the dining-room. Barred on the outside every one of them!

As she looked, a sound in the distance caught her attention and presently she saw two strange bloodhounds crossing the park in charge of a keeper. She gazed astonished, wondering at the man's audacity. He came up close to the rail which divided the park from the garden, touching his hat as though he wished to speak. She saw it was one of

their own men and went over the grass to
the railing.

"Good-morning, my lady. I thought as
how you 'd like to see the 'ounds."

"Yes, Paul, good-morning. Where did
they come from?"

"Don't know exactly, m' lady. Sir Christopher he brought them along a week ago;
told me always to bring them up to the house
when he was out of it. I 'm taking them along
now."

He passed on and Lady Javelin retraced
her steps.

All that day she was alone, and the next,
and the next. She saw her husband only at
their meals, and he spoke to her only once.
That was to forbid her having the Hobsons
or Fitz-Jameses or any one else to stay. She
did not combat his decision. She was too
miserable,—miserable with him, to see him
as he was; miserable without him, remembering what he had been.

At the end of six months she realised this
was indeed to be her life, the life she had to

face: the awful terrifying loneliness, because unutterable; the silent hidden grief of widow-hood in the lifetime of her mate.

Then followed the years—years in which Sir Christopher perceptibly lost the grasp of things, years in which little Chris grew strong and big and went to school, years in which the doctors tried their skill and talked of "retarded growth," of "symptoms of shock," of "arrested development," of "atavism," and many other high sounding phrases, which did no good to the patient or to his nurse, and which always ended with the same words, "the cure of the disease must come from within. When Sir Christopher wishes to be cured the cure will have begun."

Sir Christopher at no time expressed any wish to be cured or to be absolutely other than he was. He acquiesced in his miserable existence. "It could n't be helped," was the utmost any one ever got from him. Whether it was the parish priest, softly calling on his wandering spirit by putting forward the claims of the spirit, or the family lawyer, gently trying to reach his mind through matters of intelligent but every day affairs, or friends and relations, wise and cheerful, endeavouring to bring to his memory incidents of bygone days—to one and all came the same baffling reply:

"I don't understand you. I don't know what you're driving at. I don't know what it is you want me to do. I 'm made like this."

It was heart-breaking.

Latterly there was only one thing he knew and recognised. That was his wife's step. He would start up alert and eager with, "There she is. She 's coming now to try and get into that room." Then he would grin widely. "She can't get in, you know. I 've locked the door. She's such a suspicious woman. She's always wanting to see why I 've locked it. But I don't mean to tell her. A man must be master in his own house, don't you think so?"

And the poor bewildered listener would agree with a heart full of pity for such a

master, finding a nod in silence was enough
to keep him running on in this strain for a
long time.

"My wife's such a suspicious woman—
women are suspicious, you know. There!
She's going away now. She can't get in, you
see. Is n't it splendid fun? I 've kept that
key for years. She does n't know why I
locked it, neither do I sometimes. I forget
sometimes."

It was dreadfully sad.

And through it all Lady Javelin had a
conviction that if they could unbar that
room, and show it to him with the windows
open and the sunlight pouring in, with her
there alone smiling at him, it would bring
back a sense of the old love and the old life
and would restore him to his former self.

But no one advised this. And she could
not undo those bars alone.

So there he lived, in his two rooms downstairs, with his bloodhounds outside his door
and a man within call, obsessed by one idea,
which idea spread like a disease through him

mentally and physically. His powers became atrophied from want of use, gradually he lost all power save the most elemental. He could still eat and sleep; he could still appreciate a bed and a bone.

His brain softened, and then, a long time afterwards his poor body died. And when that was dead, Mr. Dolphin had the iron bars loosened quietly at night. And when it was buried, young Chris had the door and windows flung open to the light of day, and found no reason why they should ever have been closed.

PART II

THE ELEMENTS

There are four different states of the elements:

Their complete intermixture in which Love alone rules and Hate is excluded.

When Hate penetrates, this homogeneous world-sphere becomes separated into the individual things until the elements are completely parted from one another.

And out of this separate condition Love brings them again together until full union is again attained.

The Principles of Empedocles.

CHAPTER VII

THE VERNAL EQUINOX

THEN followed years of blessed peace,—
years when the tension of the strain
and the terror and the heart-break relaxed;
when no dark corners of the house resisted the
shining of the sun; when friends from far and
near came frequently and kept the hospitable
doors continually on the swing; when inter-
course was possible with intellects keen to
exchange ideas; and when in this healthier
atmosphere, the tired body, soul, and spirit
were rebaptised into a new life.

And the new life was young. Christopher the
eleventh re-freshened everything: his mother,
his uncles, and his aunts, their manners, modes,
and morals. And for ten years they seemed
to live as in a vernal equinox and loved it.

At the end of ten years, at the mature age of twenty-six, Sir Christopher fell in love and knew himself to be a man with a strong desire for matrimony.

He had been in love before, in and out again several times over, as becomes a warm hearted youth; and each time had taught him something fresh, leaving him with the knowledge there was still more to learn when the right woman should appear.

When she appeared, he recognised her at once. She was his equal.

Her name was Crystal and her age was twenty-six. She had been at "Lady Margaret Hall" the same time he had been at "The House," so that Oxford claimed them both. She could beat him at billiards, though allowed he was conqueror at tennis. She could listen intelligently on every subject under the sun on which he chose to discourse, and she treated him sometimes to ideas of her own, which were obviously not the result of copybook platitudes learnt in her youth.

She was the one woman in the world created to be his mate.

There was only one point on which he had the advantage of her, that was in the possession of £. s. d. She was penniless, but that was neither here nor there, since he had enough for both.

Crystal adored her Christopher, not for his £. s. d., but for his personality, including his brains. It was the intellectual romps in which they were able to indulge, rather than the physical games, that quickened her blood, quickened her wits, quickened her spirit, till she tingled with pleasure at the knowledge that above and beside all else her man possessed what the French so rightly call *esprit*.

And Lady Javelin watching, wondered at them both—how long it would last, how soon it would end.

Also she wondered whether Crystal, this new sort of girl, would prove the same sort of woman as those others who had written their names in the Javelin history book, and whether — whether? — Lady Javelin seldom answered that note of interrogation even in thought.

Then one day this new sort of girl, who was staying in the neighbourhood, came to see her, not dressed in her best, not supported by her mother, not driving up in a family carriage, but in a short tweed skirt, and the latest tweed hat. Accompanied by a lot of dogs, she was ushered into the hall.

"I want to have a talk with you. May I?"

That was what she said, and proceeded to give her commands to the dogs that they should behave in her absence. Then she put her hand through the elder woman's arm and drew her towards the stairs.

It was a long time before either of them appeared again. When they did the girl whistled gaily, and the scuttling of many feet proclaimed instant obedience. She waved her hand smiling to the lady in the doorway, who turned back into the house.

Lady J. returned to her little room upstairs, conscious that her thoughts were in a riot.

None of them smoothed out quite as complacently as before her talk with that girl. She sat down and pulled over her embroidery silks as though trying to match one against the other; in reality she was trying to match her ideas with a new set of specimens lately brought to her notice.

They did n't match and they would n't ever match, she saw that. Being an artist as well as a woman, she knew the advantage of a contrast in colour, and applied it forthwith to her point of view.

The girl was in love with Chris. There was no doubt about that, but it did n't make her jump impetuously at the chance of being his wife, it made her wish to know just what she was undertaking. She wanted to have a full understanding of the family history, if she was to enter that family, and she did not content herself with the gossip that no doubt would be told her if she gave half a hearing. She came straight to the man's mother, to the woman who rather more than a quarter of a century ago was herself standing on the brink of the unknown, to the woman who had weathered such storms as beat round the harbour of matrimony, and could tell, if she would, of those hidden rocks as it were wise to beware.

The doubt in the elder woman's mind had been just this: how much to reveal, how much to conceal. Should she let this girl take her chance as she herself had had to take her chance without any special preparation or warning, or should she tell her that in the Javelin history there had never been a woman who had played an ignoble part, only that and nothing more?

The saying that, had been voluntary; more than that had been involuntary, yet she had said it. She could n't help it. The girl had somehow led her on to tell her all she wished to know, even to some of the things written in the Javelin book. It was due to the fact that the Rector had the key that only the outside of the book had been shown.

Many women's names were in that book,— women who had suffered but had never com-

plained; women who had endured but had
never run away; women from all parts of the
land, from the north; from the south, from the
east, from the west; unknown to each other;
living generations apart; and yet united in a
virtuous bond of silence.

Crystal had thought quietly for some time
after hearing this; then she looked up smiling.

"But why? Why should they cut themselves off from human sympathy?"

"Because they were really fine characters."

"You are a very fine character, but your
case was known to everybody. That made
it easier for you?"

"In a manner, yes."

"Silence is a mistake. It's because women
have banded themselves together in this con-
spiracy that it takes so long to right their
wrongs."

Lady Javelin drew back. "Are you, do you,
go in for women's rights?"

"Why, yes."

"Oh, my dear!"

"Equality, you know, nothing more. I

don't mean to fight, but I believe women are perfectly equal with men. Don't you?"

"Not exactly equal, dear. There always must be a difference."

"A difference, yes, but the difference does n't necessarily make for inequality. We are equal and we know it, but it has always suited the male hitherto to consider us as unequal and inferior. This century is the dawn in which the poor dear will have to be undeceived."

Lady Javelin winced at "the male," though conscious of trying to appear *au fait* with the subject in hand.

"I suppose, right through that book," eyeing the red and gold cover, "there is no mention of a woman's happiness being secured through a man's tact?"

"I don't seem to remember one."

"Both in tact and judgment we are of course man's superior, as he is ours in force and energy. It 's when you get the two at their best set in battle array, that the fun begins."

"My dear, I don't think battles are the least funny. They are very degrading."

"Dear lady, not half so degrading as being a door-mat. Is it cheeky of me to talk to you like this? I won't if you 'd rather not, but it 's such a pleasure to find somebody of another generation who does n't draw down the blinds in one's face when one's mind speaks naturally—with the glass off, so to say."

The elder woman smiled at the flattery. "One need not be a door-mat. There 's surely a medium between that and a fighting force."

The girl shook her head also smiling. "Once a door-mat, always a door-mat, on which by-and-by the family will wipe its dirty boots, while it will change into clean ones to go and visit elsewhere. I know. I 'm twenty-six. I 've seen."

Lady Javelin put down her work in her lap.

"You are very young."

"Twenty-six."

"I know, but that 's very young—to me.

I 'm forty-six, and for many years of my life
I 've felt a hundred and six.

"That 's because——"

"Yes?"

"Nothing. I don't like to say."

"Do say. You think I 've been a door-
mat?"

"No, I know you have n't."

"Nor a fighting force? Then I 've been the
thing between?"

"No. You have been, you are a fighting
force; but you have n't wasted your powder,
you 've known when to cease firing. The
self-control necessary has told upon you.
Now you will grow young again."

A shake of the head.

"Yes you will, and I shall help you. You
will help me to be wise, I shall help you to be
young. Is that a bargain, mother-in-law to be?
If so, we will seal it with a time-honoured
custom!"

The girl and the woman kissed, and smiled
each at the other.

CHAPTER VIII

A FAIRY-TALE ENDING

THE move had begun, the move from Javelin Hall for the lady who had reigned there twenty-seven years and more, and who was now moving into the dower house at the other end of the park.

The young couple had gone off on a long honeymoon, leaving her temporarily in possession, leaving it to her judgment entirely, to her knowledge, and to her sense of honour, as to what things moved with her and what things remained behind.

Everything she had found in the house belonged to the house of course, but everything brought into the house through her taste and skill she was to consider hers to take or leave just as she pleased.

"DARLING MOTHER,

"I want you to have everything you want to have, because I know you will never want to have what we would n't want you to have, and tell old Dolphin to make you comfortable first, and see that everything is right for you, before he begins our papering and painting. We shall dart round to you the moment we come home but that won't be for a long time yet. Crystal sends her love, the real thing straight from a warm and bubbling heart, she says, and not the conventional apathy of a conventional daughter-in-law.

"Ever your devoted son,

"CHRIS."

This letter was in Lady Javelin's hand as she went round the house tying labels on to the furniture that belonged to her. Every room had been visited and everything was ready to go next day.

She handed Mr. Dolphin the list, then took it back from him, hesitated, and added the word "cradle," folded the paper in two, and went on talking while he put it in his note-

book. Then she went upstairs with a disagreeable lurking feeling of guilt.

Everything she had brought into the house
she was entitled to take out and she had
brought that cradle, that is her husband had
bought it at a sale in the long ago days when
for her to wish for a thing had been to possess
it, and it had lived in her room ever since,
filled formerly with toys and cushions for the
tiny Chris to play in when she wanted to have
him with her and yet to keep him quiet; since
then, since the day Chris had turned out the
toys and ordered the cushions to be burnt,
she had used it for hats. It was a Jacobean
cradle, and the hats in it were guarded from
dust by the cot cover she had worked in
imitation of an old English design. It was all
hers. It absolutely belonged to her; even
the old "Punch" tied on the top of the hood,
sitting astride and playing his broken cym-
bals, was really hers. That is, she had bought
it for little Chris and it had always lived
there. She could n't part with it. She could
not leave this thing behind. She tied on the

label with a double knot, arguing all the time with an imaginary Crystal.

"You see, dear, it had always been in my room. The servants thought it was mine—in fact it was mine—I mean it is mine—but of course if you and Chris feel you would like to have it—" she left a blank, hoping in imagination that Crystal would say, "Oh, no, we don't want it a bit. I like a muslin and lace arrangement, all soft and fluffy." That is, of course, if—when she had imagined as far as that, she imagined herself just giving the cradle a touch with her foot and saying, "Oh well, if you don't want it, it does very well for hats," and having discharged her conscience, she would then change the conversation.

The next evening she was going to bed in her new room in the old house, and she hardly felt lonely or strange, for there at the foot of her bed stood the cradle and "Punch." She set it rocking: she was a woman of forty-six and had been a widow for years, yet she smiled in her sleep, though awake she felt like a thief.

By-and-by the couple came home, radiantly happy, overflowing with the milk of human kindness, which made them completely charming to their neighbours, friends, and relations.

Word was soon passed round as to their chief characteristics. Sir Christopher was clever in an intellectual fashion, very clever. If Sir Christopher said a thing, it was worth listening to and attending to. He was a man of brains. He had read a lot and thought a lot. His wife emphasised this opinion of him by constantly referring to him as an authority. "Chris says" or "Chris thinks" fell off her tongue a dozen times a day, and the atmosphere in which they lived got impressed and imbued with Javelin thought and ideas.

"Lady Chris," as she was soon familiarly called, to distinguish her from "Lady J.," was witty. This reputation was easily established by the fact that a clever man like her husband was obviously amused at her, and constantly laughed delightedly when she spoke. Therefore the rest of the world laughed when she spoke, and admired what he ad-

7

mired, so that the popularity of the young couple was as assured as had been the popularity of his father and his mother in the early days of their early married life.

And thus things continued till after the birth of the first and second babies, which babies had lovely bassinettes in which to lie and sleep and coo, in their white and dainty nurseries, and a still more lovely cradle in which to rock and romp and play, when they went across the park to visit grannie, whose little boy had grown up and left her with an empty cradle and a dear old "Punch."

Lady Javelin at the dower house was happy as the day was long. She got up in the morning feeling happy, and she went to bed at night feeling happy. She was visited by all the hosts of people who flocked to the hall, and flocked on to her to tell her what they thought and felt as well as to find out what she thought and felt. And the praise that she heard on all sides of the reigning lady gave her pleasure beyond the usual pleasure felt by a mother-in-law for her son's wife, because this mother-in-law dearly loved her daughter-in-law as her daughter-in-law loved her.

Such harmony seems to belong only to the millennium, and in thinking of it afterwards, Lady Javelin detected the first false note as sounding on her ears the day her sisters came to stay with her after staying with their nephew and their niece.

What they said was unimportant, for they were not brilliant above the average; but on the waves of the air they made an impression, the impression that Christopher's wife led him by the nose. They did not put it as baldly as that, but they each managed to convey the idea, and the idea rankled sufficiently for Lady J. to contradict it at first in gentle fashion. After a day or two, she admitted that if it were true, it worked very well, as no one could be happier than Chris, and no one of the younger generation of married men was looked up to with greater respect or had a surer footing in the County.

The sisters then showed themselves in their

true and separate colours. The eldest said
"of course, if you are satisfied, there 's nothing
more to be said, but for my own part I like
to see a man rule in his own house.   However—"   She never got further than the
"however," because at that point her younger
sister always seemed inspired to state her own
views forthwith, and did so without delay on
this wise:

"It 's a very good thing. Man is meant to
rule the world, and in return to be himself
ruled by a woman. If he 's married and that
woman does n't happen to be his wife, trouble!
Dear old Chris will be a success just so long
as he works with Crystal and not against
her."

Lady Javelin hated to hear this said, as one
does hate to hear an obvious truth stated
with a false air of overbearing originality.
She looked at her younger sister reprovingly,
though horribly conscious there was nothing
.justly to reprove. The sister's eyes were
cast in another direction so the look was
wasted.

This small incident, though pushed out at
the moment, came back into her mind later
on when the millennium seemed rolling away
into the past.

Meantime Chris was developing intellectually. Besides being a devoted son, husband,
and father, besides filling all his obligations as
a landlord, a magistrate, and in this year of
grace, high sheriff, he read and worked and
thought and schemed, to make manifest an
idea that had taken root in his brain, and was
being carefully nourished that it might pro-
vide fruit for the world when the world was
ripe to receive it.

He would hardly speak of this idea—it
meant too much to him. It absorbed him at
times. He was like a man living in a dream.
And when people noticed his absence of mind,
along with his presence of body, then, through
Crystal, his wife, would follow quickly the
words: "He's so clever you know. He's such
an awfully clever man. He's probably working·
out a problem for the benefit of mankind,"
followed by awed admiration and silence.

It was this very cleverness that seemed likely to become the stumbling-block to the happiness of Christopher's mother, Lady J. Not that she was unappreciative of brain power, far from it, but she knew and understood the difficulties attached to the possession, unless the power of mental balance was equally strong.

She watched Chris expanding in one direction with pride, she saw him contracting in other directions with sorrow, not so much on her own account as on account of her silent daughter-in-law.

This daughter-in-law had been true to her promise. She had helped to renew the youth of her mother-in-law, and the overflow of gratitude on the one side, mixed with the genuine love that wrought the miracle on the other, made their positions as agreeable as they were unusual.

Thus it is possible to be dimly aware of the different points of view of the women of a family when the man of the family, in the fulness of time and in the plenitude of his powers, adopts not only a different attitude towards them individually, but starts regarding them collectively from an aspect so changed, that either pity for his mental blindness, or glorious admiration for his far-sighted range of vision, springs forthwith into being, and charges the atmosphere with electrical currents, of which he unconsciously becomes the storm or centre.

When this particular Sir Christopher Javelin had attained his thirtieth year, and had up till then fulfilled all the high hopes maintained of him, it was generally supposed that in his case, at any rate, the end of the fairy tale would prove to be true.

"So they married, and had lots of children, and lived happily ever after."

Such an ending is fitting to fairy tales. In the world of fact, the end is usually a long way off from the time when two people first lived happily together in the bonds of matrimony, but, as the happiness lessens in the lives of the characters, so the interest not infrequently deepens.

CHAPTER IX

MILLY

AND if you had your choice, you that are going to be married, would you choose that your life should be happy or interesting? It can seldom be both. There are cases which preserve the ideal for some of us to look at, if we may not touch, but they are rare, and bring us near to tears when we see them in their beauty.

Well, a man will generally choose that his life shall be interesting, a woman will probably choose that hers shall be happy; and this love of interest mates with a love of happiness, and lives side by side, cheek by jowl, night and day for a week, a month, a year, or even for many years. Then comes the little friction, when the interest grates upon the happiness, or the happiness perchance is thought to be hindering to the interest, and the one wants to work and live with the other, while the other wants to work and live alone.

How then? Do you wish at that point to shut up the book and have nothing more to do with the tiresome people who are not content to rock their little boat in the calm waters of the harbour, tiresome people, who wilfully adventure forth into the wild waves of the open sea and, worst insult of all, manage the little craft themselves, calling not to you for help, ignoring your advice of a pilot?

If so, "Good-bye." The rest of the story is not for you.

Sir Christopher Javelin in his thirtieth year knew that his life was overflowing with happiness, knew it so well, had breathed the air so long, that he had accustomed himself to believe the thing for which other men and women will barter their souls belonged to him by prescriptive right, would live with him always, no matter how treated, how neglected.

Happiness would never divorce Interest. That was as certain a thing to be relied on as a man's point of view. Happiness could not exist without Interest, any more than the female could exist without the male, also a man's point of view. Happiness could be relied on to stay in his life whatever Interest might do.

Therefore in his thirtieth year Sir Christopher decided that Happiness, that soft and feminine thing, might be trusted not to interfere with the harder and masculine Interest, which was calling to him out of the *Ewigkeit* with a voice not to be disobeyed. He answered gladly, cheerfully, with an exultant thrill that betokened in the future a more interesting happiness than had yet been his to attain.

And this interest was to be a great interest, a universal interest, nothing small, and mean, and petty. It involved large difficulties, hard work, and enormous courage. It was nothing less than the shape of the world.

At different periods in Sir Christopher's

life he had unconsciously prayed an unorigi-
nal prayer, in which he fervently thanked
God he was not as other men—due, not so
much to the overflowings of a grateful heart,
as to the keenly valued appreciation of his
own originality in the thoughts common to
men.

From his earliest youth he had been taught
that the world was round. He had affected
to believe it, feeling all the time within himself that such teaching was foolishness, and
waiting with the patience of a born scientist
for the day when he could prove the falseness
of such a doctrine.

This idea had lain dormant through the
greater part of his life, but it always had
existence in his brain. He had pandered
outwardly to the round and popular belief,
kicking inwardly at a world he knew, but
could not prove, to be flat.

His larger interest in life first showed itself
by his clearance from his room of all childish
and feminine trifles. He turned out his wife's
work-box and his sons' playthings. He kept

his door shut and he put up a large "Silence" at the end of the hall leading to his passage. Then he felt he had made a beginning.

It took a week or two for his small sons to understand that their father's room was no longer a happy hunting ground where lions and tigers roamed under and over the furniture, but they did learn and speedily took tickets for a "prairie" where the sport was better.

It took almost a month for their mother to remember she must not dash into Sir Christopher's den with all her silly ideas and spread them out before him, and rant, and rave, and smile, and laugh, as she foolishly talked them over with him. Foolish? Yes, no doubt it was foolish, but then she had always done it ever since they were married, and it was dull remembering to be wise when there was a certain excitement in being foolish. Still in time she too remembered and began keeping her ideas to herself. Wisely?

The man worked hard. He pored over books and papers. He bought a typewriter and made a horrid mess. He got a stoop from the shoulders and a frown between his eyes. He lost the *joie de vivre* himself and soon regarded the laughter of others, as "the crackling of thorns under a pot."

He too kept his ideas to himself. They were shut fast in his brain as he was shut fast in his room. He disliked going out amongst the ignorant people of the world. They jarred on him more than he could bear. This inward consciousness of a superior knowledge for which as yet he could offer no proof, only produced an outward irritation, difficult to allay in the atmosphere of error which enveloped the material world. "Some day," he would say to himself, "some day I shall be able to teach what I know."

Then suddenly a strange thing happened.

He walked back with his Cousin Milly to the village one evening as he had done a thousand and ninety-nine times before. Nothing strange in that. But on the way he listened to her with different ears, and he looked at her with different eyes, and he found her altogether different—not yet like the apple in the Garden of Eden—but altogether different. That was the strange thing.

He returned slowly full of profound thought. The shape of the world was interesting to Milly; Milly shaping the world would be interesting to him.

He himself—A flat world. And Milly!— It made him giddy to look over the edge of things.

He went back and sat down in his den. This profundity of thought, this sudden discovery of an interest shared, gave the man a headache. He sat inert and miserable the following day. His wife came in and spoke to him. He did not answer; he felt too ill. She laid her hand on his head. It was cool and nice. He begged her to keep it there. She stood beside him where he sat, putting first one hand and then the other on his tortured brow. Once or twice she thought of leaving him, but he asked her to stay. She also said something about a nurse, and later on about fetching the doctor. He shook his head. "Not bad enough for that." Woman-like she did n't seem content and "went on at him" about having them both. He murmured, "Thank you, but I don't wish it."

"Well I do," she said and left the room.

Left the room, left him alone, left him when he was in pain. She did n't care. She did n't care for him, nor for his ideas, nor for his sufferings. She left him alone just when he wanted her. He heard the telephone bell ring and rang his own to ask the meaning.

The doctor had just received the message and would be at the hall in a few minutes.

"I don't want the doctor, who sent for him?"

"Her ladyship, some little time ago."

"I won't see him. You can say it was a mistake. Do you hear? I won't see him!"

"Very good, Sir Christopher."

A motor horn soon made itself heard in the drive. A bell pealed, and steps crossed and re-crossed the hall.

Sir Christopher went out and faced the doctor coming in.

"I 'm all right," he began with an attempt

at a laugh. "It was n't really necessary to send for you. I!"

The doctor nodded and went up the staircase two steps at a time.

Chris thought it odd and rather rude, but went back to his den and to work. As he worked he felt the need of sympathy, understanding sympathy, not so much with his physical headache as with his mental schemes. This understanding sympathy he could have from Milly. Milly only lived in the village. It would do him good to walk as far as the village.

Some two hours later on his way home the doctor hailed him.

"Congratulations, Sir Christopher! A very fine little daughter with a fine pair of lungs is waiting for you at home."

"What?"

"Yes, that's what you'll find and the mother as well as possible. Good-bye."

Sir Christopher stood still, dazed with the news. It was n't fair to surprise a man like that. His wife might have told him. What business had women to go and do things so suddenly, without a word of warning? It was n't fair to the man.

And the man so unfairly treated walked on, no enthusiasm in his step, no anxiety in his mind, no palpitating excitement in his imagination at his wife's silent achievement, no rush of desire to see his new daughter. A wall of fact surrounded him, the fact that his wife had left him when he had a headache. He could not clear this wall at a bound.

Poor Chris! His mother met him at the door. Her eyes were bright as though tears stood in them. She kissed him without speaking.

Of course every one knows it 's a royal time for women when a baby is born in a house. How they fuss! How they enjoy the whole situation! From some men's point of view it 's a purely feminine matter with a good deal of hysteria attached to it. The man is far better out of the way, till the bill comes to be paid. Thus argued Sir Christopher to himself after his daughter's arrival.

8

He had not argued so on the birth of his eldest son. His pride and his joy were triumphant that day when he saw Crystal with a little, funny, red face tucked into her arm. Then, because he too had suffered—for her, he had knelt with tears of thankfulness beside her and felt he could never love her or comfort her enough for all she had been through— for him.

But then that was the first and a boy. This was the third and a girl.

And he had been so proud and happy all that first long time of Crystal's convalescence. It had n't seemed long to him because there were things he could do for her. He had been very busy over some plans which he wanted to see finished by the time she was well, that she might have a surprise. Thus in the bond of sympathy they lived and delighted in living.

Then came the second son to strengthen that bond, and then Sir Christopher began to get tired. He thought they had done enough for the human race and said so. His wife failed for once to agree with him. She said it laughingly, but he felt there was an undercurrent of strength in her that might sweep him off his feet and into a large family if he did not take a very firm stand.

"A family of two," said Sir Christopher, "is quite enough in these days. One more than necessity demands, and we can't afford a large family. Besides I hate large families. I think they 're indecent."

"Poor darling!" His wife had laughed again, "that 's only because you come of a race that—" she paused, "that 's so blue bloody it has always existed on a thin line of one. I should like to have a nursery and a schoolroom, both going hard, till we 're quite, quite old."

So, in course of time, with a little skill and a good deal of tact, she accomplished a daughter and sighed in silence that this arrival was not ushered in with a peal of bells or a beat of drums, feeling it incumbent on her to try and make up from the beginning for the scant notice accorded by the head of the house to the only Miss Javelin born in a hundred years.

CHAPTER X

THE VOICE OUT OF THE "EWIGKEIT"

AND when "Lady Chris" came downstairs again after her third retirement she found another surprise.

It differed from the first in that it was not so pleasant, though it had its points in that it was interesting. The surprise was Milly. The interest was in the surprise.

That any man, any sane and intelligent man, could take up with Milly, could spend hours and hours and hours in talking things over with Milly, could rush away out of the house the minute he'd swallowed his breakfast, and only return when permitted by Milly, that any man could do this, would have surprised the Lady of Javelin Hall, but that

Chris should do so amazed her beyond the power of words to describe.

She looked at this feminine cousin with quite new eyes, saw, too, at a glance she could never resemble the apple in Eden, and felt first relief, then contempt. Thus women are hard to please. She knew then there must certainly be some well hidden charm to account for this curious state of her family affairs, and Crystal at once prepared herself for a voyage of discovery into the recesses of Milly's mind. Until she had searched and found the jewel of fascination, she could only maintain a negative attitude of pleasantly noticing nothing.

For many months she had been training to keep her ideas to herself, now she must apparently live with her eyes half shut. Soon no doubt her ears would prove too good at hearing, and then, with senses purposely dulled, she could no doubt be laid on a shelf, wrapped in tissue, or used as a family doormat, just as convenience demanded.

While indulging such thoughts as these one

moment, Lady Chris took herself to task the next for allowing her imagination to play when conscious that her body was still weak. She put off speaking to Chris until she was really well, until she was sure of saying the right thing, in the right way, at the right moment, forgetting he might not be the right man to hear it at any time.

Then the usual thing happened—she spit it out suddenly, on the spur of the moment when temporarily disturbed.

She had asked Chris to come back in time to see some people who wanted to be shown the gardens after tea. He promised to come, but failed to appear. Crystal took them round, seeing them halt at every corner hoping for a glimpse of the master of the house. She apologised for him, and finally saw them go with peevish joy on her part and a sort of fretful gratitude on theirs.

Then came Chris. And this is what he said:

"Sorry I could n't be here sooner, but Milly wanted me to stay."

The wise woman in Crystal bit her tongue

between her teeth and held it firm. The man proceeded.

"I tried to get back for tea, but the muse was going strong, and I could n't interrupt the flow of inspiration."

Through her teeth Crystal said, "What inspiration?"

"Oh, I forgot you do n't know! She's writing poetry, beautiful poetry. She 's so full of ideas. It comes streaming forth at times, I hardly dare breathe; yet I dare n't move for fear it would break the spell."

Teeth and tongue were freed.

"Who is 'she'?"

"Milly."

"Sounds rather dull for you. I did n't know you liked poetry."

"Not the usual rubbish, but this is different, very different. You can feel her soul in her face."

"I suppose you mean 'see.' "

"Yes, see it and feel it. She 's wonderful!— but I 'm sorry little woman if this makes you cross."

"I'm not cross. It's too silly to be cross about."

"What is too silly?"

"Why the whole thing."

"What old thing?"

"Sorry you're deaf. I didn't say 'old thing.' I said 'whole thing.'"

"Pity you drop your h's. Do you mean Milly or your lawful husband?"

"Both of you—one's just as silly as the other. What do you want to go tearing down there for every time you get an idea in your head? What——"

"You know perfectly well why I take my ideas down there. I get them sorted out into shape and then typed."

"I can type."

"Yes, but you are much too busy. You've got heaps of things to see to for the house and —and—the children and everybody. I'm not going to add to your labours. Now Milly is more or less an idle woman, a leisured woman any way, and she has very much the same ideas as I have, specially about"—his voice sank—"about the shape of the world. Talking to her is like talking to oneself. She feels the same as I do about lots of things. Still if you insist on making a quarrel about this, of course——"

"Good Heavens! A quarrel! My dear man, you 're quite old enough to go your own way without any advice from me. If you think you 're wise to do what you 're doing, you do it. I shall never quarrel with you about any woman on earth—I 'm much too fond of you—certainly not about such an anæmic one as Milly."

The mollified expression on the man's face, which had appeared at the words, "I 'm much too fond of you," gave way immediately to one of bitter resentment as Crystal finished speaking. He said nothing, but he looked as a tigress might look if danger attended her cubs. With a rigid face, white with anger, he walked to the door.

"That 's the limit," he said quietly, "I discuss the question with you no more."

"All right. She can't help being anæmic,

you know. I don't suppose she wants to be.
It 's in the blood. I did n't make her so!"

"I heard what you said."

"I said she was anæmic."

"You said she was an anæmic worm."

"Never!"

"I heard you."

"*Jamais de la vie!*"

"You said you would never quarrel with
me about any woman."

"Because I am too fond of you!"

"And then, speaking of Milly, you said
'Certainly not about such an anæmic worm.'"

"One! Dear goose, one!"

"It 's all very well now to say 'one.' You
said 'worm' at the time."

"One! I never said worm. I never thought
of her as a worm, but now you suggest it,
she is ra——"

The door banged hard, and loud, and fast.
The woman on one side had gained some
knowledge, the man on the other had lost
some sense of humour.

Once upon a time a Frenchman was called

to order by his wife. He remonstrated and finally defied her. His wife tapped the table at which they were sitting and said quietly:

"*Bien Monsieur; moi aussi.*"

The story goes that it had the desired effect, and the Frenchman to all appearances became a loving and devoted husband, so that his wife had no future cause to complain.

Love is a beautiful cord by which a woman can hold a man, but if one little strand of Fear is woven invisibly into that cord, it lasts longer and wears better.

Lady Chris held her man by Love alone. She would have scorned that little extra strengthening strand, just as she would have scorned the meretricious airs that gloss a coarse and vulgar mind. Therefore Chris had no fear of his wife, therefore his story is longer than the Frenchman's.

He—Chris—was greatly perturbed after banging that door, and the perturbation lasted and increased day by day. And day by day he felt himself to be getting further and further away from Crystal, and nearer and nearer to Milly.

And day by day he was conscious of the shrinking of his happiness along with the accession of interest. But the interest belonged to the spirit of adventure and the spirit of adventure called to him out of the *Ewigkeit.*

The thrill of discovery was his, the discovery that the world was flat and that marriage was a mistake. Whether it was the discovery of the first that helped him to the second, or the discovery of the second that helped him to the first, and which was really first and which was second, he neither knew nor cared. They were two simple facts in his life that had to be faced.

But during this turbulent epoch, facing these facts, he was not alone. One stood beside him, one with dreamy, dewy eyes, one of soft, poetic speech, one of quiet and gliding movements, one whose plastic brain was on fire to prove what he knew, and what she through him believed. This one was Milly.

In taking Milly for his guide, his counsellor,

and friend, he dropped, automatically as it were, the companionship of his mother and his wife and his boys. These things belong to a world that is round. There is no place for them in a world that is flat. In a flat world only Milly could reign.

So in his new-found wisdom Sir Christopher put Milly on the throne, and she became his intellectual consort.

Like to like. The voice out of the *Ewigkeit.*

CHAPTER XI

THE STORM

AND for four flat-footed years this state of things continued. Which time, weary and dreary, was but as the heavy calm before the bursting of a brilliant storm.

The name of the storm was Billy.

CHAPTER XII

BILLY

IN a far distant country, a long way off, a
man ceased working, for his work was finished. He lifted up his head and listened. He
heard a voice calling. It called and called.
The man answered and sailed for home.

On the voyage he met and talked frequently
with a clever brain specialist, whose curious
knowledge of human nature made him interested and interesting. Amongst the "funny"
cases he spoke about was one of a man
who had died of the sulks. Rather than
give up sulking this man had become blind
and deaf and dumb and densely stupid,
partially paralysed in body, with a heart
as hard and cold as his brain was weak and
warm.

When the specialist was called in, he had prescribed a change of mental atmosphere. The patient rallied his forces and showed fight. He was told kindly, but firmly, he must change or he would die.

He preferred to die. He would never change. And die he did of a fit of the sulks prolonged over a dozen years.

"He was——"

"My uncle!"

"You don't say so? I was going to add he was a rich man with a lovely wife.''

"My aunt."

"Really? This is very interesting, and had a son and heir, houses, and land and everything a man can want, except the power to enjoy them. What was the name of your uncle, if it's not impertinent?"

"Sir Christopher Javelin."

"That's so. Fine old name, some superstition attaching to it, I fancy."

"Yes, the curse of a blessing rejected."

"Ha! No curse like it!"

Then they drifted into less personal matters

and later on exchanged cards when leaving the ship.

The man who had finished his work in a far distant country, went home to see his only sister Milly.

She expressed great delight at his arrival, but called him William. She excited his sympathy on her behalf as well as his interest, for she seemed involved in a difficult situation requiring the comfort of a man and a brother. This made William glad he had arrived. He sat up late into the night listening to details of the position, not an uncommon one by any means in the country he had left, but assuming an uncommon interest when the man's own sister and cousin were entangled ever so slightly.

"And there's nothing wrong, William. You may be sure of that. But you can't get ordinary people to believe it. Just a case of a man wanting more sympathy than he can get in his own home. Crystal, of course, is an excellent wife; not a thing against her. She looks after the house, and the children, and

9

the village, and does everything she ought to do; but she is n't intellectual. She can't understand that a man wants something more than just the material comforts of life, especially a clever man like Chris. He 's full of ideas, you know, original ideas, and I fancy they clash with Crystal's very prosaic temperament. She 's a dear thing but thoroughly conventional."

Brother William smoked in silence. As a man he sympathised with a misunderstood. husband, as a brother he thought Milly's attitude unfortunate—for herself.

"I fancied," he said slowly, "from various rumours that reached me, they were most happily married."

"At first, oh, at first, they were blissful! In fact, till the last baby arrived. I really think it was that that upset poor Christopher as much as anything. They had got two boys, and he was quite content. He wanted nothing more, but no, she must have a large family. You know what those very healthy women are like, never satisfied unless they are peopling the world in all directions. So she insists on having a daughter, being the sort of wife that must have her own way or else makes a row. Poor Chris said to me after the christening, 'I 'm sure I hope she 'll be satisfied now, but there 's no pleasing some natures.' That was the first idea I had of what the poor man was feeling. It was after that he began coming here so often, thankful, I believe, to get away from a discontented woman, and children who did not interest him.''

William took his pipe out of his mouth as though to speak, changed his mind, and put it back in silence.

The unspoken thought was this. "Takes a clever woman to make a man a father against his will.'' After that he kissed Milly and went to bed.

Next morning he saw Sir Christopher Javelin walking up the garden path and went out to meet him.

" Hullo Chris!''

"Hullo Billy!''

The two men, close of an age, stood scan-

ning each other. To an outward observer
there would have appeared to be ten years'
difference between them. One looked five
years more than he ought, the other looked five
years less than he was. One had the effect of
always stooping and looking in, the other the
effect of stretching up and looking out.

They talked till lunch time, when three
people sat down as a matter of course. No
invitation had been given that William knew.
He wondered.

After lunch Sir Christopher showed Milly
a paper and asked her to type it for him. She
took it at once out of the room. Sir Christopher followed her, and William with his eyes
rather wider open than usual heard a door
shut firmly, though not actually banged.

He waited in an attitude of surprise then
picked up his hat from the hall and went out.
He went first to visit his aunt, dear Lady J.,
and hoped secretly he might meet his cousin's
wife also. But luck was against him. Then
he walked on to Lady J.'s sisters, aunts by
courtesy, and paid them his respects.

From Milly later he heard that Lady Javelin was away at the sea with the children, and
would not be home for a week.

"Why was Sir Christopher not with them?"

Well really, could he expect a man to dance
attendance on his family all his life! He,
William, had indeed been living out of the
world too long for society's ways and manners.

Poor William!

He went up to town to see some plays, and
hear the latest music hall jokes and songs, to
tide over the days before the Lady of Javelin
Hall should return to her own.

There was no disguising from himself the
small excitement her existence unconsciously
produced in him. He liked to think there
was a woman in the world he had yet to meet,
who was somewhere near his own age, quite
near his own hearth, who would have a prescriptive right to call him by his Christian
name, and who might make some demand on
his spare time, his spare energy, his spare m—
no she would hardly do that, for of course she
was very well off. Any way, he was glad he

had saved some cash to enable him to enjoy life to the full, when he had found a playmate with whom he could play.

Underneath his high moral rectitude he hoped—it really was almost a hope—that Lady Chris would know how to play. The delirious sensation of possibly once again playing with fire rose up only to be suppressed.

She was his cousin's wife, the mother of a family, the Lady of Javelin Hall. Forbidden.

She was returning the day after to-morrow.

To-morrow!

To-day!

The situation was simply full of romance, looked at like this,—a neglected wife, just considered good enough to take the children to the sea, while the clever husband stays at home and writes articles on the shape of the world with a (clever!) woman, who is also a cousin; a young man between thirty and forty, longing, nay yearning, to act as chivalrous knight to some distressed fair one, and lay his hand and heart in front of her dainty feet.

Place—A garden beautiful as Eden; and in it the three historic fruits—the apple, and the pear, and the rotten medlar.

Time—Present.

Was there anything wanting? Only the acquiescence of the neglected wife. That should not be difficult to obtain—in William's case.

It was her mother-in-law who introduced him to her. He called about five o'clock the day after her return, and found the two ladies together.

"O Billy!" said the elder lady, "I must introduce you to Lady Javelin. Crystal, this is Milly's brother you have heard us talk of."

They bowed each to the other, grave, yet curious.

"What very brown eyes, like a dog's," thought the lady.

"True blue," thought the man and murmured some politeness, smiling.

She said, "Will you have some tea?" still attracted by his eyes,

As brown in hue as hazel nuts
And sweeter than the kernels.

He would have some tea, and he would talk, and he would see the children, and he would play with them, and he would see his aunt home across the park, though it was a good mile out of his way back to the village. He would leave a good impression behind for the personal benefit of "the neglected wife."

He laughed sardonically to himself when next alone. Anything less like "that" he had never seen.

A woman who looked like a girl, moved like a girl, spoke like a girl, and a girl in the full possession of her powers, mental and physical. A woman who was a girl at heart, and a d—d good-looking one—a wife, but not neglected.

Impossible with that figure, that colouring, that air of hers, the carriage of her head, that way with her. No, no, no. His eyes fell on Milly. He suddenly felt sorry for his sister. She must be under a mistake. A man would

have all his work cut out for him to keep even
with a woman like his cousin's wife.

"Good old Chris. Wily old bird!" He
smiled to himself, "and he had thought—ass
that he was—he had thought——"

The depression that accompanied him to
sleep, the knowledge of having built on ideas
and not facts, the consciousness of the possible
chance of his lifetime knocked to bits suddenly
as it came within reach, mixed in his dreams
and spent itself before morning.

With the dawn he ceased to worry. With
the full sun he rose an optimist again. Life
was worth living, and he was glad he had come
home. Milly evidently wanted him. Yes he
was glad—for Milly's sake. Cheating liar!

There was a dinner party at the hall; lots
of people were bidden to meet him. He and
Milly went together and enjoyed it. His
cousin's wife added to her more apparent
charms the elusive charm of a perfect hostess.

The most fastidious could be pleased. Billy
had not considered himself fastidious till
now. In his time he had appreciated a

bar-maid of respectable family, a chorus girl
whose people had estates in Ireland.   Sad
cases both of them.   He had been interested,
at the time.   He remembered now—and
wondered.

The best, the very best, and only the best
of which he was capable, would be of any use
here.   To be friends with Lady Javelin, a man
must have cut connections with all things
mean and base and low.

Billy put his foot down on various traits
in his character, with intention to use them as
stepping stones for the future.   Heigh-ho!—
but was n't he glad he 'd come home.   And
was n't Milly sorry!

As day by day passed, William's interest
increased.   The articles on the shape of the
world were shown to him freshly typed and
clipped.   He thought they emphasised poor
originality of thought.   They roused no enthusiasm either for themselves or their author.
He spoke to Milly on a delicate subject in a
way that made her think him rough, and she
said, "if only you understood."   He owned it

was what he was trying to do; what he would leave no stone unturned to do, if thereby he could satisfy his reason in justifying the situation.

And every time he saw Lady Javelin, he was more non-plussed than ever. He thought her adorable, and wondered how soon he could tell her so.

He loved to hear her mentioned. He would twist the talk so as to make somebody bring in her name; not a difficult thing to do. It required no tact. People were ready to talk.

The two ladies known as the "Anti's"— the elder because she was Anti her own sex, and the younger because she was Anti the other, gave him food for much thought.

Aunt Patricia spoke to him of the situation, not because she wanted to, but because "she felt she ought." William liked women to have principles and encouraged her warmly.

She deplored to him Crystal's inability "to keep her husband's affection." She said it quietly with a pink spot in either cheek, because it was such a dreadful and mortifying statement to make, but then it was the truth. Any woman once blessed with the priceless possession of a good man's love should prize it and guard it as a thing sacred and above all else in the world. She could speak because she knew. Her knowledge, as William was aware, was long ago founded on a rapturous three weeks' engagement to a Captain Fitz-James, whose pre-nuptial death had precluded for her that riper experience and maturer judgment which comes to those versed in the ways of matrimony.

Aunt Patricia's experience of men was a singularly happy one and brief as it was happy. Because she had known and loved Captain Fitz-James, she loved all men. They could do no wrong in her eyes. At the back of any apparent mistake, Aunt Patricia scented a woman. No man would ever go wrong of his own accord. He was always the innocent victim of some miserably wicked or beautifully designing hussy, and a married woman who failed to manage her own man, was too contemptible to be considered in any way.

William understood that young Lady Javelin had already entered this category. He recognised she was beautiful; he hoped in the thoughtlessness of the moment she might be wicked or even designing; but miserable? Never, if he could help it!

He said anxiously, "I hope, Aunt Patricia, that you don't feel Christopher has been got hold of by——by any one answering that——"

"Oh, dear, no! He's much too clever! A man must have female society. One knows that. One does not expect a man to behave like a woman. He wants a little fun and a little sympathy sometimes, and if the poor dear does not get it in his own home, well, you know, men always will be men."

"Quite so, and that sort of thing is always more exciting when found in somebody else's home."

Aunt Patricia nodded. "I can't tell you how I admire your sister Milly. She has simply stepped in and saved the situation. She, a cousin, supplies for him what the wife lacks. I can't say more than that."

William nodded. In those few words she seemed to have given him a history of the world, and his silence betokened grief mingled with admiration.

On the way home he glowed with the consciousness that whatever he did, he would ever and always have Aunt Patricia's sympathy. Likewise the other aunt's. Aunt Judy's life glowed also with an admiration that was permanent, not temporary, but it was not for him or his. His sex existed in Aunt Judy's eyes but to be of use to her sex. There was no other *raison d'être* for the male.

Consequently if Billy could justify his existence by supporting "the woman's cause," he would in turn have an ardent supporter in the most belligerent member of his family and generation.

Billy determined to so deal with an individual case that Aunt Patricia's words should echo proudly for Aunt Judy thus:

"He, a cousin, supplies for her what the

husband lacks. I can't say more than that."

Billy at the moment had no desire she should.

CHAPTER XIII

WILLIAM TALKS WITH HIS AUNT J.

SIR Christopher Javelin's articles on the shape of the world pleased him and Milly enormously. They were a pleasure to write, a pleasure to read over together, a pleasure to type, a pleasure to correct, and a pleasure to see in print.

They were a source of pleasure, combined with amusement, to the neighbourhood. The neighbourhood liked having a celebrity in its private midst, whom they could speak of with much familiarity when at a distance. They loved hearing somebody in Scotland or on the Continent saying to no one in particular:

"What odd things this man does write. Who is he? Does anybody know?"

They in the neighbourhood knew and

squenched their eagerness with poorly acted indifference as they drawled slowly: "Odd, yes, I suppose he might strike people who did not know him as odd. But we know him so well. We live only a few miles from the Javelins. And he's clever, you know. All his family have been clever, or odd, as outsiders might call it. Of course, he's most original!"

Billy read the articles and defined them as "rot," but then he lacked the refined mind of his sister, who felt that reverence for brain power was another of the things that William did not understand.

Milly's pleasure in Sir Christopher's printed pages was the more commendable in that she herself was suffering from a prolonged stage of rebuffs. Her poems were sent off to evening papers and monthly magazines with a buoyant regularity that betokened success past, present, and future, but they returned with equal regularity, so that her joy in life was not her own peculiar offspring's popularity with the public, but the vicarious and altruistic joy

of a noble soul watching another's happiness
in a progeny with whose birth she had nothing
to do, but whose after-training had been
lovingly delivered into her care.

Milly moved on a plain far beyond Billy.
Yet Billy ventured to interfere with Milly.
He spoke to her one day not so much as her
protector and brother, as master of the house.
It was a most sympathetic speech both in
manner and matter. It was a revelation to
Milly of the coarse primitiveness in which
most men's minds are moulded. She shuddered
and shrank from him. He was quite ruthless
and told her really very unpleasant things,
that no nice woman would like to be told.
He spoke slightingly of platonic friendships
and was otherwise rather rude. Milly hated
him and brokenly repeated all he said to
Christopher.

Sir Christopher called the next day on
Billy and was shown into the smoking-room
with some ceremony, where he addressed the
scowling occupant as William. They had a
warm quarter of an hour alone with each other,

in which the brother played a noble part, while the husband, taken at a disadvantage and having nothing prepared on that score, was soon in a wild and sorry plight.

"I 'm not here to defend my own character in any capacity," said Sir Christopher later, "merely to defend your sister from your monstrous accusations. As my coming here in no way interferes with you, and gives your sister some poor little pleasure in life, I must beg of you to cease meddling in a friendship that is evidently beyond your ken and to ask that as long as I leave you and your affairs alone, so you will have the goodness to leave me and my affairs alone. Is that a bargain?"

Billy hesitated, then he said firmly:

"It is," and they shook hands.

The devil had shaken the frying-pan and the fat was in the fire.

The immediate result of this conversation was that Sir Christopher burned to do something for Milly that should distract her thoughts from her disgusting brother and also turn them full-tilt into a new and pleasanter channel.

He wrote to the editor of the local paper, marked it private, and enclosed a copy of one of the rejected poems. He asked the editor for his true and honest opinion of it. He threw in his own view but admitted he might be prejudiced. The poem was unsigned.

Curiously enough, the editor's opinion of the poem agreed absolutely with Sir Christopher's. He considered it of unusual merit. He would be very pleased to publish the poem on the usual terms. Was he correct in surmising it to be the work of Lady Javelin? In which case should it be signed, or would her ladyship prefer it to appear anonymously?

William also was suffering from the overheated state of the atmosphere. He too was burning to make up to a woman for the abominable behaviour of her husband. He wanted not only to comfort her, but to be a comfort to her. The chief obstacle at present was his entire ignorance of whether his position

of comforter would be acceptable to the
lady.

She might not need comfort, or—horrid
thought—she might have already been sup-
plied with this household want. Intolerable,
but possible!

In this torture of suspense he turned his
steps to the dower house. He must know the
worst, and if there was a worst, it would most
surely be known by Lady J. He dreaded yet
longed to hear.

He passed through the garden but found
it empty, on to the house, and was ushered
into the little room off the drawing-room.
Lady J. was sitting with her work in her lap.
Her daughter-in-law was reading aloud something that interested them both, for a scarcely
smothered sound of annoyance greeted his
over-strung ears.

He sat down and talked with intent to re-
move that annoyance and knew to a moment
when it left in disgust. Then he proceeded to
be amusing and interesting, so that the
younger lady laughed, saying he was as good

as a play. He liked that. It would do for a beginning, but he would love the day when she found him a comfort.

The children came in to see their grannie and were left by their nurses to walk home with their mother. Billy choked down his disappointment, and played so well with the children that he hoped their mother would feel sorry at walking back with them and not with him. Then she would arrange differently another time.

After they left, he stood kicking the toe of his boot into the gravel without knowing he was doing it.

An angel spoke to him, and for the joy of hearing such words again, he stopped kicking, stamped the pebbles back into place, and said, "Sorry, what did you say?"

"I said that 's a woman in a thousand!"

"You don't mean it? Is she, is she?"

"A dear! I 'm devoted to her."

"How ripping, Aunt J. She looks rather nice." But he was conscious of a blow inwardly. If his cousin by marriage confided in

his aunt, where would his chance be? He
could not rid himself of the desire to loom
large in the younger lady's eyes. He wanted
to be "something" to her. He lied even to
himself. He knew he wanted to be everything.

"Billy! You've known Chris all your life.
Tell me, do you see a change in him or do
you find him just the same?"

"I think he looks much the same, older of
course, but we're all marching on."

"Of course. Let us sit down." They had
got to a shady corner of the garden where was
a wide low seat. Billy knocked the ashes
out of his pipe, encouraging sign that a man is
ready to listen.

"Billy, sometimes I'm afraid. I see signs
of his going like his father."

"No, Aunt J., no."

"You think not? Pray God you're right,
but——"

"What about his wife?"

Lady J. threw up her head. "That's
where she's so splendid. She won't allow

there 's anything wrong, and yet she knows,
she knows there is."

"You know I 've had a row with Milly?"

"You have n't? Oh, Billy, my dear, how
brave of you! Then you saw?"

"Saw? They never prevented my seeing!
A furious row; told her what I thought of the
whole proceeding. She told him, yes Chris,
and he took up the cudgels in her defence.
So he and I then had it out. He has forbidden
my interference in his affairs so long as he
does not interfere with mine. I have agreed
to the bargain—an evil one—still I 've agreed."

"I don't believe there 's anything wrong, you
know, not really, but they are so absorbed in
themselves that they don't see how it strikes
other people. Besides——"

"Yes?"

"It 's made him—Billy is it fair for me to
say this even to you? But you don't know,
you can't know what it is to see your only
and beloved son turning his back on—on—
He used to be one's ideal of everything that
one wanted him most to be. His devotion

to me—well, you remember." Lady J.'s voice trembled, and Billy put his arm through hers and held her hand in his red, warm grasp.

"He made the happiest marriage. She insisted on learning the family history before she said 'yes.' So she married with her eyes open. And he adored her, was proud of her, proud of his boys, proud of the place, his position. He was very useful in the County, did a lot of unpaid work for everybody, kept his youth and health and spirits in a wonderful way. Then I saw a change after the little girl was born. He took no interest. Indeed, Billy, will you believe it when I tell you that he never saw Crystal for a week, and after that never once sat and talked to her, or made much of her, or treated her as anything but a tiresome woman who had gone out of her way to annoy him? That at a time when a woman wants all the petting she can get."

The red warm hand comforted Lady J. It was so sympathetic and strong. "And Crystal made excuses for him, till my blood boiled. Yes, though he was my son and she was only my daughter-in-law, I have been on her side all through.   Then, of course, came this Milly craze, when he has n't eyes or ears for any one else; when I, Billy, his mother. I am less than nothing to him—less than nothing!"   A tear splashed on to the big hand covering the little one.   Lady J. put her pocket handkerchief on it with "Sorry, dear boy, and I can't say a word, for he is near to hating me.   I think he does hate his wife, really hates her, and the boys too."

"Really!"

"Yes really, I do.   That 's the difference in the two women.   When he loved Crystal, he did everything well.   He was a man to be proud of.   She made him love everybody else and everybody loved him.   He was open hearted and open handed.   Now he hates most of us, he looks the picture of misery, and is such a miser you can no more get a shilling out of him for any one than you can a kind word or a caress.   Do you wonder that at times it seems more than I can bear?"

"Dear Aunt J.," Billy squeezed her white

hand against his lips and kissed the fingers with an engagingly absent-minded air.

"I am sorry," he murmured, "I 'm dreadfully sorry. How long has all this been going on?"

"Since Babs was born. Dear little thing, she 's four years old now and her father has never kissed her once, never played with her, never treated her as his daughter at all. Billy is n't it like——"

"No, my dear, no—not a bit." Billy might have been talking to a young girl, his voice was positively paternal. "It 's just a phase, you know, it 's bound to come right in the end. I don't believe when a man has a good mother and a good wife, he ever goes straying for long, but of course it looks as if Milly is at the bottom of the whole business, and if so——"

"I don't agree. I think it just happened that Milly was handy, but I think anybody would have done just then."

"The wrong woman at the right time *versus* the right woman at the wrong time—one often sees that Aunt J. It accounts for half the worries in the world. What would you like me to do, dear?"

"I don't know! I just had to speak to somebody. Perhaps I shall be sorry, but it 's so hard to keep silence feeling that a little plain language might do good. I don't mean you can put things right. You 've had a row already with Christopher."

"Yes, I 've harassed him, and embarrassed her, and generally been told to mind my own business."

"I 'm sorry, Billy, you should come home to this."

"That 's all right, Aunt J. Glad if I can serve you at any time. How would it be if, if I—took to paying court to the lady at the hall? Eh? What? Should you approve?"

"I should like you to be nice to her. She 's very, very lonely. Won't have her own people often. Does not want them to see. You might perhaps go and call sometimes. It might wake Chris to his duties, but I don't

know. It 's a very difficult case. One dreads
to interfere lest one make matters worse!"

"Has she ever asked for help?"

"Never!"

"I mean not only of you, of any one?"

"I think not. She won't allow she needs
help. It 's only I who admit that. It is she
who comforts me, when I 'm unhappy about
Chris. She says it 's quite natural for him
to want to go off occasionally. I think she 'd
like him to go big game shooting or something
of that sort."

"H'm, has she got a hobby?"

"Well yes, she has. I can't tell you what
it is."

"Oh, yes, Aunt J.!"

"No, dear boy, I can't really. I ought not
to have told you that she had one. I found
it out by accident, and she 's so very sweet
about it, but I can't tell you or any one."

"Righto! But if she 's got a hobby, it 's
an enormous help you know. It saves her
from being stranded."

"Crystal is n't the sort of woman to be

stranded. She's not a bit like me. When my best was taken away, my life was wrecked utterly. If Crystal's is snatched from her, she'd make you think she had n't lost anything that was worth having."

Billy was silent because his tongue was in his cheek.

He got up and walked Lady J. back to the house. He said good-bye, leaving a warm and grateful spot behind him in a poor bruised heart, and took himself home, a bundle of ramping curiosity.

CHAPTER XIV

HE DREAMS OF A PALACE

BILLY could not rest till he had discovered Lady Javelin's hobby. Secretly he was jealous of the unknown. If Sir Christopher was making her unhappy even passively, he, Billy, saw his chance of becoming her consolation. He did not wish to be baulked by "a thing." If she were the sort of woman to be engrossed in things rather than people, it would not suit him so well. But how get into her confidence?

As primitive man with a rough idea of chivalry, he would have liked to ride up to the hall some morning and say to her:

"Fair lady, I adore you. I am going to take you away from your ogre of a husband, and if you will come with me, I will bear you off to my palace and other delights." While, forthwith, in imagination he saw them whirled into a happiness of the evermore kind of order in books.

As civilised man, living in rather cultured times, he felt the stern necessity of diplomacy. He deprecated the delay this entailed, but the excitement thrilled his blood, as the consciousness of possibly justifying his existence at any moment, was now born in upon him daily.

He began with the children. He met them in their walks and he bought them penny toys at the village shop. When the boats would not swim, he used a knife that made them swim. When the joy of wooden horses and tin soldiers was exhausted, he filled his pockets with sweets and encouraged the boys to climb all over him in search of such things as their little souls loved.

"Cousin Billy" became a household name in a very short time. The children's mother was solicitous. "Cousin Billy" was much too kind. "Cousin Billy" must not allow himself to be tyrannised.

William, full of Machiavelian schemes, played his part very well. "He was fond of boys, very fond of them. It was really a kindness after his rough, selfish life in foreign parts, it was really a kindness to let him inside that Holy of Holies, an 'Englishman's Home,' and to let him romp freely with the Englishman's sons, and to let him pet the Englishman's daughter, that dainty, white piece of goods, who had never been kissed by her father."

When his free run of the house had been fully established and he was known to be "always there on the children's account," he stumbled on Crystal's hobby in the most natural way in the world.

He found her again one day reading aloud to her mother-in-law. Both women had a bright colour, and their eyes had the light of excitement in them. They looked at him as he entered and laughed. He did not know if he was meant to feel as an intruder, but he had no intention of being so obliging and said ruthlessly, "What 's up, Aunt J.?"

11

"Shall we tell him, Crystal?"

Lady Javelin looked him up and down provokingly. "You can tell him if you like," she said, "on the way home."

Thus Billy walked back with his aunt that evening instead of remaining with his cousin, but it was all a step in the right direction.

The secret came out with a jump.

Crystal had written a play, and it was going to be acted in a real theatre, by real actors and actresses. And, it was only a curtain raiser. Still it had been taken, that was the thing, and it was going to be acted, in London, in the autumn!

Billy was silent from mingled motives. Lady J., sure of a sympathetic listener, talked on. "This, of course, is what has helped her to be so splendid all this long time. She has written short stories for magazines ever since she was a child. Not under her own name, no. She had got two names, one is suitable for the *Sunday at Home*, and the other is n't."

Lady J.'s tone seemed to apologise for her enthusiasm as she added after a pause: "It 's been my great excitement, Billy, acting audience for her. She read me one of her plots one day when—when other things were very bad, and it took me out of myself. She wanted to see the effect. She wanted to know if anybody could be moved by her way of writing. She moved me. Then she told me what pen and ink did for her. Pen and ink, plus brains, and her dear courageous soul have kept us both from misery. My happiest times are when I slip off into her room and we shut the door and she says, 'Not at home,' and we live in a world of her own creating, with people of wit and talent, who make us laugh and sometimes cry, who give us thoughts and ideas, and worry us never. It does not want publicity and a theatre, to make me proud of Crystal!"

William was amazed. He had not thought of this. Brains?—always a questionable addition to a woman meant to be loved. Publicity?—except such as a man could give her—No. He mentally shook his head, though outwardly he said something complimentary. Then later the rebound seized him and he

thought of her two signatures. "One is fit
for the *Sunday at Home* and the other is n't."
This from Lady J.! It really was rather astonishing. It revived those vivid imaginations
of his regarding a palace and other delights.
It, well, metaphorically speaking, it turned
him inside out and upside down.

A woman with two names of the pen meant
a woman with a two-fold nature. The domestic Crystal, who looked after the house and
the children and wrote stories for the *Sunday
at Home* must of necessity be a different
Crystal from the one who required and used
a second and a different name when writing
for the week-day world.

Was Christopher the man to satisfy a two-
fold nature? Had he such a superabundance
of vitality, health, and spirits, that he could
give, and give, and give, and not be the poorer
for the giving?

And if he could give, could he also take
generously? The one, William knew, implied
the other. The man or woman who knows
how to give, knows how to take. Had Sir

Christopher this knowledge? When he thought of him with Milly, he said yes; when he thought of him with his wife, he said no.

And if this were so, then the chances were all for Mr. Billy William, the man who in his own opinion knew jolly well how to give and how to take.

First he would find out, why she did it. He was now at the stage when a name is superfluous. Was it to still a hungry heart, or to feed aching pride; was it to make money, or for the love of fame? That is what he would know.

And he only had to wait a day or two and then he learnt it all.

She wanted money to bring a water supply to a certain group of cottages in the village where they had none nearer than the pump. For generations the pump had been visited by housewives, who had carried every drop of water in slopping cans and buckets for the daily washings, cookings, etc., of cottage necessities. Crystal had seen a woman staggering back to her home just before Babs was born, a woman who had quite enough to carry just then from Dame Nature without any additional burden, and Crystal's heart had gone out to her and she had told Chris of the daily want in that corner of the village. But Chris, with his larger brain, was too busy shaping the world to bother about cottages, and said in his lordly way, with the rare understanding of the male, "she would no doubt be wanting tiled bath-rooms next in every shed on the place." And when the subject was pressed, he also said, "if she were so keen on another water supply, she could pay for it herself. He would have no objection and would put no obstacles in her way." Yet he, as her husband, knew she had not the means to do this thing.

William thought he had heard of women saving out of the housekeeping money wherewith to embark on projects of their own. He said so to Lady J. when she told him of the water scheme, and then Lady J. reluctantly admitted such an easy and common arrangement was not possible in this case. Because?

Because Sir Christopher gave no allowances, housekeeping or otherwise, for Crystal or the children. Everything in life, he said, could be purchased now-a-days under one roof. He refused to be "bothered" any longer with money affairs. He would have a deposit account in one place, where Crystal could order everything—for the house, for herself, for the children.

The place he selected was the Army and Navy Stores, in which incidentally Milly had shares. She, Crystal, might clothe the village from there if she pleased as well as get everything else. When he said "everything," he meant "everything." Naturally it would include her gowns and her hats and her shoes and, of course, wedding presents. Did she not understand the meaning of the word everything? No bills would be paid in future from anywhere else. So she could please herself about orders. He intended to get his own things entirely from th███s and what was good enough for him w█████ enough for anybody.

William put back his head and roared. He thought Lady J. was "pulling his leg." He honestly did not believe what she told him and said so.

"But Aunt J. for a woman—surely half her delight in life is shopping. I understand that going from one place to another and comparing the different wares is a large asset in a woman's daily and hourly happiness. Isn't that so?"

"Yes, I think it is."

Pause.

"She does not look as if she dressed from Victoria Street!"

"Not yet. She has managed to do with things already ordered. That's why you found us looking so pleased the other evening. She had received a cheque for her own work. Now you know what it means for many people if Crystal can make some money."

"Dear Aunt J.!"

It dawne█████e man listening to her what the mothe█████have suffered silently before she could talk so, even to him, of her son.

So "she" was doing it for money. All the easier for him to help her.

He helped her almost immediately with the programme for a concert. She found out he was musical, because she had one day just come in from riding, when he called, and the children had gone off to a party. So while she changed, she heard the piano and his gay and quite untrained voice singing:

I will make you brooches and toys for your delight
Of bird's song in morning, of stars' shine at night.

She thought it charming and begged him to continue when she came downstairs. He was only too well pleased. He loved the sound of his voice when set to music. He required no pressing. He was wholly untrained and too willing to oblige. He sang the same words again straight at her, continuing with:

I will build a palace, fit for you and me
Of green days in forest and blue days at sea.

His voice was sweet and powerful and absolutely true. He sang by nature, and as though he loved it. They talked of music and he said he could sing better if somebody played for him. She suggested Milly; he feared Milly was n't much good. Would n't she try? He was sure she could if she would.

The result of such trying was a concert in the near future stage-managed by Billy, who promised himself as accompanist for all performers if she would accompany him. Thus they practised a good deal together. Tickets sold at high prices. Success was assured. And there was a fat nest-egg for the new water supply in the village.

CHAPTER XV

COMES THE DEVIL

IT was after this people began to talk.

Milly's poem on the "Friendship of a Square Peg for a Round Hole" came out in the monthly edition of the local paper, signed with her full name and address. So there was no mistake. Each verse began with the words;

> What can be the end
> For us two, O my friend?

Though all understood the situation, nobody seemed to care very much, in spite of this reiterated appeal, what kind of an end there was or even whether there was any end at all. They found the other friendship in the family far more interesting. A thrill of excitement pervaded the atmosphere of Billy which some-how left Milly untouched.

Milly could be clever enough and intellec-tual enough to act as secretary for her cousin, that talented man, Sir Christopher, and yet raise nothing more than a mild surprise in the eyes of a very few; while Billy need only dance attendance on Sir Christopher's wife, for all tongues to wag, and all hearts to feel a pleasurable emotion, which generally pro-duced a smile. Everybody agreed that Mr. Billy William adored Lady Javelin. He had not mentioned it to anybody, still they affirmed they all knew it the night of the concert.

Several compared notes, and "That song, my dear, settled it once for all."

"The song about the palace? Yes, we thought so, too."

"No, not the palace, though that was clear enough, but that other one,

'Come to me, Sweet,
On silver-girt feet.'

I forget how it goes, but you know the one I mean."

"Yes, I forget how it goes, but I know the one you mean."

Thus did each speaker seek to deceive a listener. Not a soul at the concert but remembered the rest of that audacious song of Billy's, not a soul. Had they not encored it, and when he had sung another, had they not raised such a clamour that Lady Javelin had smilingly nodded to him with "You'll have to repeat it, Billy"?

Everybody heard her say that; everybody saw with what alacrity Billy obeyed. Everybody felt like amateurs suddenly mixing intimately with professionals. It was thrilling, his voice, his manner, his general air, and the consciousness of every wicked word he sang coming straight from his heart with intention to pierce another.

It was with bated breath that any one afterwards admitted remembering his "Strangle my soul in thy kisses' perfume." They said it in softest whispers, as though thoroughly ashamed of repeating such words, and yet they had encored them in public and would encore them again every day of their lives, if Billy would give them a chance.

Billy gave them every chance. His blood was up. He became horribly and wildly reckless. He sang this sort of song any hour of the day or night. He sang them to the married and unmarried. He caused fearful flutters in the local dove-cots; he did and said things that nobody else did and said, with impunity; yet he was forgiven. Was he not home for a lark, poor man?

And larks he could have had for the asking in any number, but he only wanted one, the one that sang highest in his heaven and was for him—*verboten*. The dreadful enticement of this for Billy home on the spree: his cousin's wife, attractive and beautiful, trying to do what was right under difficult circumstances; husband-cousin, otherwise engaged without let or hindrance. Is it any wonder Billy whistled with the thought in his heart:

> "Man is the fire, woman is the tow,
> Comes the devil and begins to blow."

The devil was blowing hard, poor Billy!

He bought a present one day, but found it would not be acceptable. He changed his tactics with the most artful diplomacy. He said he wanted to give it to his Aunt J., because she had been so kind to him since he came home. He only wanted her, Crystal's opinion of the thing as an *objet d'art*.

His success was wholly undeserved. She blushed. Blushed! Billy eat her up, so to say, in one blissful gulp.

"I adore you!"

"Wh—wha—what are you saying?"

"I adore you."

"William, you must n't!"

"No I know, but—" he ground his teeth and then he—well he hugged her like a bear.

As soon as she could move, she stood up a crimson and offended goddess.

"How, how dare you!"

"I love you."

"You must be mad!"

"Yes—mad about you."

"Will you go, please."

"If you wish, but I shall come back."

"William!"

"Well?"

"Think of Chris."

"Does he think of you?"

"That doesn't matter."

"Ho!—doesn't it. Damn 'im!"

"Sh——"

"I'm glad you know. I should have died if I hadn't told you."

"I think you'd better have died."

"Do you?" He came closer to her, his face just above hers, without actually touching her. She backed, but found the edge of the sofa pressing her hard. It was a case of standing rigidly still or else flopping backwards in an undignified heap. She stood rigid.

"Do you wish I were dead?"

"No, of course not."

"Do you wish I'd never come home?"

"No."

"What do you wish?"

"I wish you 'd go away."

"No you don't, you darling! You don't!"
He was behaving like a bear again.

"Th-th-think of the servants, the children,
the——"

"Damn the lot!"

She went out of the room and away upstairs. She never wished to see him again.
Never!

She waited to hear him go. He never
went. She only heard Sir Christopher come
in unusually early. He sent upstairs to ask
her to come down. She answered that she
had a headache and was resting.

She dressed for dinner determined to make
Christopher attend to her. She must make
him see that it did not do for her to be left so
much alone. She must force him, if again persuasion failed, to see that he must consider
his wife, not only himself.

He came to her door as she opened it.

12

"Look here, I 've put off dinner a quarter of an hour. I 've been talking to Billy. He 's got rather a good idea for my next article on the shape of the world, so I 've asked him to come back and we can work it up together. You don't mind do you?"

"Yes, I do mind. Come in here."

She had her say, she gave him the hint; she told him enough and more than many husbands would care to hear—and Sir Christopher first pooh-poohed and then laughed.

She refused to come down to dinner. She would have "something on a tray" upstairs. Sir Christopher fidgeted "That was so like her!" She could see Billy a dozen times a day if she wanted to, and now when he, her husband, for once wanted her to be pleasant to this man, she made ridiculous difficulties, as she always did. Her headache was n't likely to be any worse now than it had been all the afternoon. He really must beg that she would come down, and as for her thinking herself too attractive for Billy's peace of mind, he, Christopher, would see to that, she could

trust him. This was to be a "business"
dinner, and for once he asked her to be of
some help to him.

"Very well," Lady Javelin said, "if you
can't understand, I suppose you can't. I 'll
dine downstairs if you 'll send the motor for
your mother. If she comes to make a four,
then I will."

Sir Christopher said, "Heavens above!
What is the matter with these women?"
but he went into his room and rang the bell.

They sat down at a small round table, the
two women facing each other and the men
between.

Billy's attitude was one of almost servile
courtesy. In speaking to his aunt and to his
cousin's wife, the charm of deference was
greater even than his charm of voice, which
was always considerable.

Christopher watching, wondered whether
his wife had taken leave of her senses when
speaking to him upstairs. There was obviously
no foundation for the scandalous things she

had implied, if she had not said. He had been quite right to insist on her coming down, that he might see for himself there was nothing —absolutely nothing—in Billy's manner to which any right minded man or woman could object.

Crystal in a topsy-turvy whirl of amazement wondered, exactly like Christopher.

Lady J., watching for a chance word alone with her daughter-in-law, watched in vain, for Billy followed them into the drawing-room. His clever ideas for a review article had been jotted down on paper while he was dressing, and Christopher was now making them ship-shape for a discussion after the ladies had gone to bed.

Billy said he wanted to sing and went to the piano, one eye on his hostess. She gave him no encouragement, she was looking for her knitting.

"You 'd like me to sing, would n't you, Aunt J., dear? I thought you would, if Cousin Crystal will be so kind as to play for me."

"Sorry, but I can't play to-night."

"Does n't matter. I 'll play for myself, something wooing and cooing because I think you are both tired."

He meandered up and down through various delightful harmonies. Then suddenly, he broke loudly into song.

> "What war is this of thee and me?
> Give o'er the wanton strife:
> You are the heart within my heart,
> The life within my life."

The knitter looked up, impelled not only by the fearful noise but by some power stronger than herself. She met Billy's eyes and tried to read shame and sorrow in them, but could find neither. All manner of things were there, but no trace of sorrow. She dropped her own for fear, for fear the hardness and the coldness in them should melt before the warm fire in his.

The audacity of the man! He sang straight through from beginning to end:

> "Come to me, Sweet,
> On silver-girt feet,"

and while his aunt thanked him, his cousin became inwardly hysterical.

The game was up. He had conquered so far, for he had made her laugh. Laugh? She was shaking with laughter, he was so incorrigibly wicked, and while she shook, Billy gravely discussed the words of the song with his aunt. " 'Pervade me with a musky scent,' " I think that 's ripping; don't you, Aunt J.? One seems to smell it." He drew in his breath with closed mouth and closed eyes.

"No, dear boy, I dislike musky scent of any kind and should hate you to be pervaded with it."

He went on, "And then 'Possess me like a tune'—that 's so good. One knows people who have just that effect on one. They do possess you, don't they, Aunt J.? At least, they do me," he crossed over the room, "just like beautiful music. Do you ever feel possessed like that, my Lady Cousin?"

"Yes," she said, and hope sprang sparkling in his eyes, "when I 'm possessed by a new plot for a play."

In controlling his sudden disappointment, Billy bit his tongue, which seemed full of pain.

Christopher came in with a closely written sheet of foolscap. He was ready for Billy's opinion.

Lady J. said good-night and motored home across the park. Life was full of pitfalls. The situation, even from the little she had seen, was becoming more dangerous every day. She thought of Chris self-absorbed and imprudent, of Milly vain and weak and moral, of Crystal, that attractive buoyant personality with its healthy craving for a large family, of William, wicked, wicked William, with his warm heart, his nice manners, and his impious ways.

"If," she said sadly to herself in the motor, and left a long pause, "if—could I blame them? Could I blame them? Would anybody? Would God?"

She knew what the answer must be.

When she knelt down before going to bed and whispered "Lead us not into temptation," her mind was full of Crystal. "Deliver us from evil," seemed suddenly to mean more than the hasty patter of a lifetime. Lead *her* not into temptation, deliver *her* from evil. Don't let it be harder for Crystal than it was for me, but then Lady J. fell asleep, thankfully grateful she had never had to contend with a man like her nephew, Billy.

CHAPTER XVI

WILLIAM TALKS WITH AUNT PATRICIA

BILLY became almost as useful to Christopher as Milly. He did not spend hours of the day and night in secretarial work for him, but he flung out an idea now and again that required much thought and help from the chosen companion, and kept the two heads with their short-sighted eyes close together week after week, toiling but happy.

Not that Billy believed the world was flat, not he. He knew the world too jolly well. He knew what it was that made it go round, and keep round, and he relaxed no effort on his own account to make it spin harder and faster for his little existence in it.

He loved the world and all things in it, and the world loved him—dearly. Animals, hirelings, children, men, women, were all in sympathy together. Even his relations, even Milly and Christopher, bore him no grudge now he had learnt to mind his own business, and had ceased interfering with them. The aunts, all three, adored him. Was he not very nearly a scamp, and was it not on the cards any day that he might be a credit or a disgrace? —Nature's passport to every woman's heart.

Lady J. and her sisters were now at variance, not for the first time, partly over him. Aunt Patricia, while condemning Crystal, was upholding Christopher. It was preposterous of Crystal to give food for talk in the neighbourhood, while it was only natural that Christopher should interest himself with Milly if he wished to.

That the two cases were parallel, she could not see. Crystal was a married woman. She had to guard her husband's honour as well as her own. It behooved her to be as Cæsar's wife. She, Patricia, did not blame Billy. Poor dear man, he was home to enjoy himself, and if he found Crystal "that sort of woman," of course he took advantage of it. She repeated, she did not blame Billy, but she did blame Crystal. Lady J. tried to stand up for the absent. She reminded Patricia that Crystal was an attractive as well as a clever woman, that it really was no fault of hers if Billy's admiration provoked the comments of the neighbourhood. Somebody was always being talked about. If to-day it was Crystal, to-morrow it might be Milly.

"Not a bit the same thing." Aunt Patricia was snappy. "It passes my comprehension why you, of all people, should stand up for Crystal. It's most unnatural to take the part of your daughter-in-law rather than your son. Milly has not to guard a husband's honour. She's an unmarried woman. If she does get talked about, it's only in an intellectual sort of way, that she's clever enough to be a companion for a man like Chris. It does not hurt or injure a man in any way if Milly were to become notorious. But if Crystal, the wife of——"

"Really Patricia!" Lady J. frowned.

Judy, hitherto silent, snorted loudly, "Absolutely indecent! To hear you talk Patricia, one would think you had been educated in the year dot. You are older than any of us, we know that, but æons seem to have rolled between the spread of your ideas and ours. That thing belonging so peculiarly to your men, which has to be preciously guarded by a woman, for fear of being lost or mislaid, does not seem to me worth all this fuss. A husband's honour isn't different from anybody else's honour that I know of, and why Crystal should be supposed to nurse it in her lap all day long, I fail to see. You are so fond of thinking men the stronger sex, and yet every time you speak of them, you show the poor frail things requiring woman's support to keep their reputation at all. I never hear you say Christopher ought to be looking after Crystal, always Crystal ought to be looking after Christopher. Why? because in your heart, deceitful and desperately wicked as it is, you know woman is superior to every created thing in the world."

"My dear Judy, we know you're a maniac

on the subject of women. They are all angels in your eyes."

"Then they match your archangel men. So between us we balance the world. I'm not going to spoil Crystal's fun, not for you or anybody. If she likes to lead old Billy a dance, well let her. It's nothing to me or you, apparently it's nothing to Christopher, unless, of course, he's come to you for help! Perhaps you're a secret service agent, are you Catty-Pat?"

Lady J. bit her lip. She wanted to laugh at her younger sister, but feared to hurt the elder. She cleared her throat. "I think Judy is right," she said quietly. "If Milly and Christopher can be trusted to take care of themselves, I am quite sure Crystal and Billy can do the same." She wasn't a bit sure really, dear sweet lady, but she must be loyal to her daughter-in-law. "If you, Patricia, uphold Christopher in a friendship that some people might think unwise, you can hardly condemn Billy for having a similiar friendship."

"Not a bit similar!" They were back again

arguing in a circle, and Patricia snapped exactly as she did a quarter of an hour ago. "Milly does n't take presents!"

The air of finality with which this was said produced a momentary silence. Patricia felt she had thrown a bomb and looked now for the wreckage.

"Silly of Milly! I always thought she was silly, but if she 's as silly as that, she 's sillier even than I thought."

"Judith! Why do you advertise your complete ignorance of what is proper in these matters? I——"

"Well I would n't work and slave for any man, certainly not a blood relation, and get nothing out of it! No presents and no wages, good Lord!"

"I suppose you are aware that Christopher's wife apparently agrees with you. She is not above receiving things from young men? I know, because I happen to have seen them and remarked upon them. The answer I got from the lady herself was, 'Yes, that 's thanks to Billy.'"

Lady J. did not look up from her work. She answered quietly.

"She 's only taking care of his things for him, till he gets a home of his own. He is collecting old furniture and old china—" (Sniff from Patricia, and a sniff of quite another sort, still a sniff, from Judith.)

"Pearls are so useful in a bachelor's home!"

Lady J. then looked up. "He brought those pearls to me, and asked me to wear them for him. He would have given them to Milly, but Milly had somehow put his back up. I refused. Just then Christopher came in. Billy showed him the pearls, told him they ought to be worn continuously, if they were to keep their colour, and asked him if he would like to take them and get his wife to wear them. Later in the day I heard Crystal refuse and I heard Chris say it was very disobliging of her, as he wished her to do it. To please him, Christopher, she——"

"Aunt Pat! Run you to earth at last! I so want a talk with you. I 've been to the cottage. Not there. I followed the trail all through the village, over the river and up the mountain's height.   Despair was settling down on me when thoughts of Aunt J. diverted me *pro tem* from suicide.   Are you busy or may I walk back with you, and will you give me some tea?"

Patricia collected herself with an air of being daily sought after in this fashion and condescended to go home with William.   She never regretted it.   People rarely regretted pleasing William.   He generally made it worth while.   In this instance she gained so much of his confidence that she lost that acerbity of spirit which had marked her speech of late, when considering Christopher's wife.

William spoke touchingly of his loneliness in a far distant country, of his greater loneliness on returning home to find his only sister alienated from him, of the kindness he had received from all and sundry, especially from his relations at the hall.   It was, of course, absurd to suppose Aunt Patricia could be concerned with his affairs, still he did want to talk to somebody sometimes.

In the pause Patricia nodded. "I know, dear. I know," implying, if this was one of. the times, she was ready to be the somebody.

"Yet if I go there often, in the most natural way in the world, just to play with the children and that sort of thing, then censorious tongues begin to wag, and there's the devil to pay—beg pardon, Aunt Pat. So sorry I forgot."

"All right, dear boy! You do remind me of Captain Fitz-James!"

"Do I, Aunt Patricia? I'm so glad. He was an awfully nice chap, wasn't he?"

Patricia shook her head slowly. "I never met any one like him, never. You remind me of him more than any one else has ever done. Still of course you are not really like him."

"No." Billy moved his burden of thought with his Machiavelian schemes off himself and his own affairs for a moment, while he contemplated Aunt Patricia as engaged to a man like himself. Or rather he tried to fancy himself engaged to Aunt Patricia and hugging her as—then his thoughts settled permanently where they most wished to be.

"I wondered if you would help me, dear, kind Aunt. A word in season from you would just put matters on the right footing. They are right now—of course you 'd know that—but the right word from you at the right moment would simply dry up those censorious tongues, belonging to people who can't see a man and a woman happy together without suspecting evil."

"I 've done it, William. I 've done it this very afternoon. I was doing it when you came in. I 've always said Milly is a wonderful woman, a perfect companion for Christopher, so intellectual——"

"But it 's I, Aunt Patricia, it 's I that want help. I 'm quite as intellectual as Milly and I want companionship without disagreeable things being said by disagreeable people." They had reached Patricia's gate. Billy held it open for the aunt, then swung it to, took off his cap, and leaned bareheaded over the rail.

"Will you stand up for me and my intellectual companion, Aunt Pat?"

The lady hesitated. William held out both his hands and she dropped her skirt to allow both of hers to meet them. He pulled them slightly towards him. His face was close to hers. "We 'll mention no names, my lady Aunt. It 's safe with you, is n't it? But if you ever hear anything said that should n't be said, you 'll remember our talk, won't you? And you 'll know that only the best is good enough for your nephew William. Only the best, in the very best way, can be any comfort to a rather lonely man."

He leaned further over the gate and his face rested momentarily against Patricia's face. "Is that how Captain Fitz-Ja—no, we won't mention names, will we?"

Patricia was quite pink and she took away her hands and her face. "You are naughty," she said, "but you have the same irresistible way with you. I never could refuse Captain Fitz-James."

"Happy, happy Fitz-James." Billy's brown

eyes were almost dewy. "And you won't refuse me, will you, dear?"

"I can't do much, but I 'll do——"

"You can do everything. You can make all the difference in our friendship, if you like to. Don't force it, Aunt Pat. I would n't have you force it for the world, but if you get a chance, you might tell her how lonely it is for me, and perhaps you could encourage her not to be afraid of evil tongues. See, dear?"

He turned away, and the hand that bravely waved to him, also wiped away a tear.

It was not till much later Patricia remembered William had had no tea.

CHAPTER XVII

A PLOT, A PLAY, AND A SONG

CRYSTAL was enjoying an animated correspondence with the actor manager who was producing her little play, entitled *A Rising Man's Wife*. The actor manager wished to change the title. He suggested, *When a Man Succeeds* as being crisper and conveying a greater idea of possibilities both for the woman and the man. Crystal saw his point, but was averse from altering the principle involved, that she as parent, more than any one else, had the right to name her own child.

She consulted Christopher, that is she tried to do so. She told him she had written a small play and the people who were going to act it, wanted to alter things. She wanted to know who, he considered, had the right to the last word, the author or the actor?

Christopher said it was a matter entirely for herself to decide. If it was an alteration materially affecting her play, why she had much better not let them act it. It probably was n't worth quarrelling over, and whether it was acted or was n't acted, as it was written or as it was n't written, it would be all the same in a hundred years' time.

Even with such immense help as this Crystal was still undecided. Her mother-in-law avowedly wanted Crystal to have everything arranged according to her own wishes. At the same time she felt the manager knew what best caught on with an audience, and she wavered from day to day.

"Talking of plays, have you seen *When a Man Succeeds?*" she would say suddenly in her most society tone and manner, and Crystal laughing would aver she had n't and did n't want to, she heard it was rot; while Billy, bursting out of newspapers, would exclaim, "We must go and see this next time we 're in

town, *A Rising Man's Wife.* Sounds good—
don't you think?"

Finally the author gave in to the actor and
then later had to go to London for the rehearsals.

Christopher could not go with her. He was
too busy. He hoped she did not consider it
unkind. She must n't think he was unsym-
pathetic about her little play. He was prepared to be quite interested, but just at the
moment she must not expect him to do
anything.

His mother went. She and Crystal started
off together, feeling a little guilty, not because
there was anything wrong, but because they
were both going to enjoy themselves in a
new and thrilling experience.

William went because he had old-fashioned
notions about ladies being alone in London.
Also he said Crystal must have a man with
her when visiting the theatre. It made
Crystal feel young and exquisitely beautiful
when William talked like this, till the whole
affair savoured of the unusual, with the future

possibility of an unknown attack of delirium
if the play were a success.

The rehearsals were different from anything
they had pictured. The drab colourlessness of
the performance, the many and various altera-
tions, oppressed Crystal with a sense of wonder
that she had ever troubled to write such a
play, combined with amazement that any one
should think it worth acting.

"No one will ever want to see it!" That
was her first spoken thought, and Billy was too
dear about it. He understood exactly how she
was feeling, but he knew it was due to reaction.
After the excitement of anticipation of the
best had come the deadly realisation of the
worst. He knew and he understood. That
was the "nice" thing about Billy. He always
"understood."

One day the manager made another and a
fresh suggestion. He wanted music. He
wanted a song sung by the heroine, a song
describing her own feelings on seeing the hero
climbing the ladder of fame. He knew of
just such a song. Would Lady Javelin watch

and listen to the effect? He was sure she would agree with him that music at that particular point would be most telling.

Lady Javelin, her mother-in-law, and her cousin, Billy, agreed to the music, but objected to the song. It was silly, they thought, inadequate to the situation. Something better must be found.

The manager's patience was oozing out. He had had a tiring and busy day. He "wished" somewhat sarcastically that her ladyship could supply the song. It would, of course, be far better if the words were her own, and perhaps he could get it set to music, though the time of course was short.

Lady Javelin bowed to him. Probably she would be able to send him something that might do. Anyway she would see and let him know.

They left the theatre.

"Don't speak to me, don't speak to me till we get home! That jack-a-napes introducing a rotten thing like that into my play. I'll write the sort of song he wants, if I die for it."

"And I'll set it to music."

Quick and grim determination gripped them fast.

"Billy, yes! We 'll do it!"

They were dining out that night but before they went Crystal had got something down on paper that she "thought might do."

It flew off the end of her pen, scribbling on her knee, while her maid was doing her hair.

The fascinating life of a rising man's wife
　Is a theme on which I very often dwell.
At first it 's simply Heaven, then there 's just a
　　touch of leaven,
　While finally it 's not unlike a word that ends
　　in l.

You begin so gay and grand, gazing upward where
　　you stand
　At the ladder with its many empty rungs,
And you think how all the time you will follow in
　　his climb,
　If only you keep strong in heart and lungs.

At first it 's very slow as laughingly you go
　Just gently step by step and hand in hand.
Then he gets a bit in front, and his voice sounds
　　like a grunt,
　And you pant a bit and strain a bit and so——

You get just left behind. No fault. He 's very
    kind.
But it happens in a world of little things.
So you watch him in his might, rising almost out
    of sight,
    While you wish that God would give you feather
        wings.

When he 's reached the top at last, like a sailor at
    the mast
He commands a very wide, extended view.
He can see for miles around; he can hear a rushing
    sound;
    He can see and hear 'most everything but YOU.

And you know it 's best to keep where you are and
    not to weep.
It 's best to just sit still and learn to smile.
There's a chance that, in the end, he may either
    come or send,
    If you are sweet and patient for that little longer
        while.

She read it over to Billy on their return
from the dinner. He nodded and said, though
it did not scan, it went to music at once in his
head. He carried it off with him to his hotel
and returned the next morning, humming a
tune that exactly fitted the words. It was a

catchy tune, with an echoing repetition of the last word in the second and fourth lines, which was pretty and fanciful.

Crystal was pleased, Lady J. was pleased, and Billy was enthusiastic. The manager was pleased because it was his idea well carried out, and the heroine was pleased because she saw a chance of making a hit on her own account. Therefore, the next rehearsal thrilled from start to finish and blotted out the despair of all previous days.

Everything was settled. The trio left town to return the night of the first performance.

They tried to bring Chris, in vain. He was far too busy to go to theatres. He hoped they would enjoy themselves. He would never stand in the way of their pleasure, but he must always be excused from sharing it.

He was so occupied with the controversy then raging, so he alleged, in the papers as to the shape of the world, that he did not take in his wife's literary efforts, or the nervous anticipation of possible disaster that made her courageous and silent concerning her own doings,—an artist longing for appreciation, a woman fearing a rebuff.

The night arrived and in a box the author tried to hide herself from the vacant sight of empty stalls. She and her mother-in-law and Billy sat through the curtain raiser and knew that it was very good.

The manager had hoped Lady Javelin would fill the theatre with notabilities and friends of all sorts. He did not understand her reticence in the matter. He was not disappointed in the play, but he was disappointed in her. The point about which there was no disappointment for any one was the song.

It was sympathetically sung and received great applause. For encore the charming woman repeated the words,

"And you know it's best to keep where you are
    and not to weep.
  It's best to just sit still and learn to smile—
      smile—smile.
  There's a chance——"

She paused and the orchestra continued without her, while she stood silent but smiling till the final chords, then she blew a kiss aloft, as if to the vanished hero, and said quietly:

"What a chance!"

The pit and the gallery shouted approval. The attention of the small audience in the stalls was arrested and amused. The impression of cynical patience in the heroine's life touched the cultured few and they applauded softly after their kind.

The three in the box were conscious of a tension suddenly relaxed. They sat back comfortably in their seats, glancing with pleasure and appreciation the one at the other, and presently the manager joined them, beaming and genial.

The play was a success.

CHAPTER XVIII

THE GRACES OF LIFE

THE countryside was thrown temporarily into mourning by the death of Lady Larkin, wife of the Sir George Larkin, who had taken part in the Javelin tragedy many years ago. Latterly she had been a complete invalid, and during that time Lady J. had been her best and most intimate friend.

Christopher went to see his mother, ostensibly to condole, actively to dissuade her from attending the funeral. She would only be dissuaded if he would promise to attend and represent the family, which under the circumstances she naturally supposed he would do. Sir Christopher seemed to hesitate. Lady J., in a somewhat highly wrought condition, said: "Of course, you 'll do this."

The tone in the woman's voice put the man's back up, albeit they were mother and son. He stiffened visibly.

"There's no 'of course,' my dear Mother. I 'll go if I can, but I 'm rather busy just now; a good deal of work to correct. However, I may be able to spare the time."

This opened the flood-gates. Lady Larkin lying unburied was forgotten. Other things not forgotten rushed in with whirling haste. Mother and son spoke face to face. A great, loving, wounded, tender-hearted, and forgiving nature suddenly broke bounds.

She said things she had never said before, had never meant to say. His utter indifference for years to the living, she had borne with patience and fortitude. She herself had long been of "no account" in his life. She had seen him neglect his wife and his children, and yet had not only shown no anger but had tried to conceal from him her sorrow. But the dead—to them was due all honour and respect, and her blood rose at the slight to them that his words implied.

The final and apparent cause may have been inadequate, for the sense of tremendous anger possessed her. She spoke with no loss of temper, but with a deadly precision, flying straight for the truth of things with the un-erring confidence of a sure judgment. She tried to dislodge him from that dry and impregnable rock of self on which he had lived so long. She spoke of love, and honour, and duty. She spoke of others dependent on him for happiness. Christopher seemed like a man asleep.

He merely shook his head from time to time; then—"Crystal does not care," he said with some bitterness, "women who care for their husbands' company make some effort to keep it. There are scenes and rows, no doubt, but they at least prove to the man he is of some value. Crystal has made no scene."

The sullen words and acrimonious tone revealed to Lady J. the wounded pride of the speaker. He had wanted to go his own way and his wife had not thought he was worth stopping. She had "let him go."

14

Lady J. paused before speaking. "Crystal will never make a scene," she said quietly, "she is much too fond of you, but you are making it almost impossible for her to——"

"Well, what? to live with me?" He gave a short laugh. "That 's very easily arranged. No woman need stay with her husband in these days if she does not wish to. I should be the last man to demand such a sacrifice. The decision rests with her either to go or stay. She can do as she likes, absolutely."

Lady J. groaned in spirit. This was worse than anything she had feared. The callous, cold-hearted indifference brought back to her a hideous memory ot long ago, the memory of when she had knelt weeping to the image of a man made in stone.

All the anger and the confidence went out of her voice, but having begun, she felt she must finish. There remained one thing still to say—Milly. Christopher went white to the lips.

"Milly!" he said deliberately, "my friendship with Milly is something you can never understand. I don't expect it of you. I don't expect women like you and Crystal to understand a friendship like mine for Milly, the carnal side of life is a thing apart from her."

He quitted the room and the house, leaving with full intention a stinging insult behind for the woman who had given him birth, and had dared to speak to him, Sir Christopher Javelin, of the graces of life.

Lady J. did not go to the funeral of her friend. She herself was ill. Prostration of the nervous system hid her from sight for days.

Only her daughter-in-law and Lady Cumberland gained admittance to her room. The younger woman understood and grieved, the elder understood and remembered.

Sir Christopher alas! was his father over again. *Ecce homo qui non posuit Deum adjutorem suum.* How would he end?

Meanwhile the sense of friction and irritation spread even to the village. Milly was not immune. She felt herself suddenly slighted

by her inferiors' looks and manners. She
fancied herself cut by her equals, who at times
managed to avoid seeing her. She wondered
what was the matter with the world. It
seemed a very misshapen affair that all the
cleverness of Christopher could not mould
straight. She became nervous. She hated
walking outside her own gate alone. When
the neighbours laughed as she passed, she
thought they were laughing at her. When
she saw them talking together, she imagined
herself the subject of remark. The village
became unbearable. She hinted this to her
cousin, but before she could do more than
hint, he had flown off at a tangent and she
had tried to soothe him with contradictory
expressions of her own mistake in the matter.
No doubt her own stupidity—but the fact
remained that she did not like the position.

She bore with it for Christopher's sake, till
one day she had a door banged in her face—
banged in her face, although a steaming hot
soup-can was in her hand.

She retraced her steps, set the soup-can

down in her own porch, tied a large dark
motor veil over her head, and went away
quickly up to the hall.

She walked through the house, straight to
Lady Javelin's room. She opened the door,
saw Crystal at her table surrounded with
papers of all sorts. Milly made no apology but
shut the door and said:

"Well, I want to know the meaning of
this?"

Crystal eyed her from head to foot. "Won't
you sit down," she said politely.

"No. I'd rather stand. What does it
mean?"

"What does what mean? Do sit down."

Milly sat obediently. "What does it mean
that the people dare to be rude to me? Lady
Cumberland has n't asked me to help her at
her bazaar—not that I mind. I hate bazaars,
but it shows the way the wind is blowing. No
one ever asks me to do anything now-a-days,
and this morning the Scroops banged their
door in my face. I don't know if it was Mrs.
Scroop or that horrible daughter of hers, but

one of them banged it when I took soup there,
and the other one laughed in the window.
What is the reason of it?"

"How should I know the reason of the
Scroops's behaviour?"

"Not the Scroops only. I 'll do you the
justice to suppose you don't discuss me with
the Scroops, but the others, and anyway
Lady Cumberland."

"I don't discuss you with the others, or
with Lady Cumberland, or with anybody."

Milly sat back in her chair, incredulous.

"You can't mean this."

"I do mean this. Why should we discuss
you?"

"I—I thought you would. I thought you
did. Yet there 's nothing, nothing for anybody to say. There isn't anything to discuss."

"Exactly."

Milly sat up. "You knew there was nothing
wrong? You knew that Christopher and I
were, well, all right, did n't you? You must
have known that we were—I don't know how
to put it—but different from most people."

"I rather supposed so, but—do you think it matters?"

"Matters?" Milly's face was crimson with indignation. "You don't think it matters if people do wrong?"

"Yes, yes, of course. I meant the degree."

"I don't understand you—" intellectually Milly was extraordinarily like Christopher. "I simply can't understand you. Not to mind, not to care, what is said of your husband!"

"What is said?"

"Oh, I don't know. One just feels things in the air—at least I should, if I had a husband."

"I did not know things were being said. What sort of things do you feel in the air? Do tell me!"

Milly fidgeted. "You must know there's talk. I can't explain——"

"Talk? What sort of talk? Who talks and what do they talk about?"

"Really, Crystal! I thought you at least would see the difficulties of the position!"

"But what position?"

"You know perfectly well, and I, I don't like the position!"

The natural woman, listening to this, gave vent silently to a wicked laugh, but the courteous lady of ages triumphed over the natural woman and, without a flicker of a smile, Lady Javelin said gravely:

"You have been very kind Milly, very kind indeed. By helping Christopher with his work, you have made it possible for me to do many things that otherwise would not have been done. I have been extraordinarily free, thanks to you. Indeed we both owe you a very great deal. I have never had a chance of thanking you before or of telling you how grateful I was and am. Also, I hope you won't stop being kind to Chris, because of Mrs. Scroop."

Baffled, humiliated, mortified, in the kindest manner, Milly knew not how best to leave the room. To stand up to her full height, shake hands with her hostess, and be shown the door, seemed as impossible to accomplish as to creep out on all fours.

Crystal turned to the table where lay her papers. She folded one set over another, and did not look round until the sound of a hurried movement behind her had ceased.

Once started, the friction did not end there. It was bound to re-act on the man who of set will and purpose had chosen to reverse the laws of harmony in his social life.

As Milly talked to him, weeping while she talked, Sir Christopher felt he understood why men committed suicide. The pleasure he and Milly had derived from their friendship was wiped clean out of mind by the horrid thought, "It had suited Crystal." It had suited his wife that he should be led by the nose by another woman!

The base ingratitude of man! When he and Milly had rejoiced in secret over their wonderful friendship, unacknowledged on the part of either, the trying circumstances of a neglected wife had been also calmly contemplated by both.

They had rather enjoyed feeling "a little

sorry" for Crystal. It emphasised their own
goodness of heart in that they still thought of
her at all. The ever present, though unobtru-
sive, idea of "Crystal out in the cold," seemed
to increase the warmth of their own attach-
ment—so perfect a thing, when at all times the
man says, "Give," the woman says, "Take."

Now, when Milly had wept her say, all this
wonderful beauty of perfection and friendship
was swept up in a phrase like that, "He had
been led by the nose." Poor Milly and poor
Sir Christopher Javelin! He had been led by
the nose, and it had suited his wife. There
seemed nothing wonderful, or beautiful, or
perfect, in a situation that could be so summed
up, nothing perfect except—he was not surprised at the thought of suicide. It was
preferable to living consciously with a perfect
fool.

The base ingratitude of the male!

Thoughts of a suicidal tendency ran themselves out in riot very shortly and more
permanent ideas took their place. He would
live. Sir Christopher Javelin must protect

the woman whose good name seemed in danger
from the tongues of an evil-minded family
like the Scroops.

Gratitude once more slipped in through
some unguarded chink, and Sir Christopher
felt that as long as Milly lived, he too must
live for her, even as she had lived for him.

All this delving into the deep things of life
produced a very serious demeanour for them
both. Any gaiety of spirit, surviving the
close friendship that had tied them so long, was
crushed by the importance with which they
viewed the future. To live for, not with, each
other, was a consideration serious enough to
account for the gloom permeating their en-
vironment to the exclusion of any lingering
trace of that gift of the gods—the *joie de vivre*.

The end of his thinking was when Sir Christopher knew, without a shadow of a doubt, that
Milly had come to be a duty. After that he
thought no more, he merely acquiesced. And
Milly, looking at him, and recognising herself
as his duty, showed no trace of resentment, no
sign of rebellion. She, too, acquiesced.

This prospect of perverted saintliness regarding their futures had a curious tendency to make them both rather glum in the immediate present—a state emphasised no doubt by that wretched Billy, who just at this time had a craze on him for singing or humming or whistling. His entrance to the house was always set to music; his stay in it and his exits were likewise accompanied.

The particular words that got on Milly's nerves and jarred her cousin's system were bawled with utmost frequency and drove the unwilling listeners silly:

> "But when love brings
> Heartache and pang,
> Tears and such things,
> Love may go hang!"

"Love may go hang." Billy seemed to dwell on the words as though he loved them. Obviously he had never known the heartache and pang. Why should he be immune?

CHAPTER XIX

FAREWELL

WHEN the great pleasure of Sir Christopher's life passed from the furtive and fleeting joy stage to the ponderous permanency of duty, the change seemed to influence his whole *raison d'être*.

It was one thing to slip quietly out of his own house and by devious paths find his way to the village and then to Milly's door, there to clasp hands over their secret ideas as to the shape of the world, and it was quite another to stalk forth from the breakfast room, conscious that his speedy departure was regularly reckoned on, and that the oftener he went and the longer he stayed, the better it suited his wife. There could n't be any pleasure in that.

Not that Crystal ever said such words, not

that she ever showed herself as harbouring the idea, but her persistent abstention from "making a scene" was proof to Sir Christopher that she no longer loved him and was "glad to be rid of him at any price." This was how he positively translated the negative. Acute perception no doubt helped him in his shaping of the world.

The boisterous happiness of Billy and others drove him well-nigh to madness. It was all he could do to keep his little corner of existence free from the radiating powers of Billy. He did it, but it was only done by his constantly being "on guard" against those insidious things, love, and laughter, and life. But he did it—he and Milly between them, from behind trenches of depression, decay, and death.

When Billy talked of going away because his time was up and he had got the chance of a new appointment in another part of the world, Sir Christopher confessed to a sincere relief. He was thankful the man was going. The continual abiding presence of a virile personality was to him just then an irritant than which none greater could exist.

His wife went her own way. Why, he never troubled to tell himself. He was too tired, too inert, ever to reason anything out. He merely accepted the conditions around him, as he accepted Milly. There was no pleasure in either for him. But he did not complain. He laid this flattering unction to his remnant of soul when at times it required petting—in this as in so many ways he was unlike other men. He never complained.

So he silently suffered from his wife going her own way. It never occurred to him how amusing it might have been for both if he could have gone with her nor, having long ago lost his sense of humour, did it ever strike him how funny it would be if she always came with him. No smile curled the corners of his lips; they were set firm in the gloom of fact—his wife was going her own way.

And along with Crystal went the family, the neighbourhood, the village, the social, legal, and political life of a whirling sphere.

Movement and change were represented by her whose persistent belief in a world that is round, was no doubt the chief stumbling-block to her husband's accompanying her hand in hand through it.

When the appointment in a far country was first suggested to Billy, he wrote to Lady Javelin from London and asked her what he should do. The compliment touched Crystal, though it made her smile. She knew it was the wish of his heart, yet, ignoring this, she responded only to the compliment by another.

"As you have this chance," she wrote, "I do hope you will take it, not only for your own sake in the future, but for my sake in the present. There are a few things in this world I can do fairly well, but it is dawning on me that I am no good as a lion-tamer. In fact, I am quite useless at it. Therefore go, dear Billy, while my blessing still rests upon your head, and before my own hair is flecked with grey."

Not a word, not a single word of complaint or regret for herself, only that light touch on the heavy reins of circumstance which Billy as a sportsman so adored.

He carried the letter in his pocket all day. He read it at intervals in London, though he knew it by heart, and while repeating to himself the bit he liked best, he was stopped in Pall Mall by a man with an amused smile.

Billy could not place him for the moment. His thoughts were all with that dear inefficient lion-tamer.

"You don't remember me? We travelled home together last year on the——"

"Of course! My wits were wool-gathering. How are you?"

They stood talking, then strolled on together. The elder man asked the younger to lunch with him at his club. Billy went, a vague, uncertain, indefinite idea floating at the back of his mind, that this was all arranged somewhere up in the blue, that it was part of a plan in which he was being pulled by wires. He felt no resentment, only curiosity.

Billy went home, a few days later, taking his

15

new-found friend with him. He plunged him straight into the heart of things, knowing he had been there before.

Lady J. at the dower house thought there was something familiar about that clever friend of William's. She felt as if she had seen him elsewhere, yet could not say when. He appeared to be an archeologist and studied the tombs in the churchyard as matters of interest.

Lady Javelin received him at the hall. The old Rector and Mr. Dolphin proved mines of information on subjects wide of the mark, and his visit was considered a success even by Milly when she knew Sir Christopher had shown him *the* book.

That marked the extreme intimacy of friendship; for when Billy's acquaintance left at the end of a week, his departure was regretted by each member of the Javelin clan. Their interest for him was about equalled by his influence on them, shown chiefly in the fact that when Billy went to that far country, he took Milly with him.

Years went by. The boys went to school.
The little girl grew to be a big girl greatly
accomplished. The mother wrote and published under an increasing number of names,
enjoying an existence that would have made
the lives of six ordinary women interesting:
the life of a wife with a husband of the calibre
of Sir Christopher Javelin; the life of the
mother whose natural care for her own children yet permitted an overflow for others
adopted by grace; the life of a daughter-in-law
with a mother-in-law like sweet Lady J.;
the social life of the lady of quality in a certain secure position; the romantic life, with
its invisible halo, its visible pearls that were
"only lent," and its crumpled telegram, dated
far back from Southampton, with its pencilled
words, now hard to read,—

"Good-bye. Farewell. They will not guess.
But you will know——"
Nothing more. The verse was not finished.
It was unnecessary. She knew. And then,
last but not least, her own life in the realms
of the unseen,—the life where her creative

faculty could have full play, independent of those other lives which in their turn, though unknown to them, were yet dependent on this, the life that helped those other lives to live.

While everything round him moved forward, only the sad master of this cheerful house stood still, or stepped, if anywhere, backward. He lived in the past with Milly. That kind hands had removed her physically from his side merely made him hold the spiritual memory of her tighter. "Out of sight—out of mind," was applicable, no doubt, to common folk. Sir Christopher was not common and not ordinary, that was the mistake so many made in feeling they could deal with a character so complex.

To take away a favourite toy from the average child might produce a temporary hullabaloo, after which he would console himself with another near at hand and the incident be forgotten. But the case was not parallel. Sir Christopher was no longer a child. He was hardly the average man, and he resented bitterly the interference that had parted him from Milly.

The recollection of her latterly as a duty hanging millstone-like round his neck was forgotten, the expected rebound after the loosening of the millstone did not take place. He remained bowed as before, blind to the happiness of the situation that permitted him without a word to return to his former greatness in the family concerns. He lived in the past with Milly, an even more depressing position than when the past had been the present.

And day by day, and year by year as the growing interests of the children seemed likely to encroach on his time and his thoughts, he stepped farther and farther back into the gloomy shade of the shape of the world as it appeared to him and Milly.

Never did it cross his mind that just as he in his way grieved for Milly, so his wife, in her way, might grieve for him, never. She had "let him go"—the priceless possession! She had not cared "to keep him"—this was

the result. She must just take the conse-
quences of her damned indifference.

Neither did it ever occur to him that a
woman like Crystal might miss a friendship
with a man like Billy. He had not liked
Billy and he was thankful when he had gone.
That was the beginning and the end of his
thought about him, and of Crystal he did not
think because he could never get over the fact
she had let him go when he refused to be held.

During the years that followed Billy's
friend came down once and again, though
knowing everything had been tried which
could be tried, knowing also the heart-breaking
result, that whereas Sir Christopher was
formerly blind, he now was deaf; that where
formerly he had not understood, he had now
passed to that lower stage where he misunderstood, whether unconsciously, or wilfully and
vindictively, it was hard to say. The fact
remained patent to all that Sir Christopher
Javelin was mentally blind, and deaf, and
unutterably stupid, with the dense stupidity
that betokens signs of deficiency and decay.

To the mother's cry, "Can nothing save him?" he had shaken his head. "Nothing but an earthquake. It will have to be a gigantic upheaval to move the crust of years."

And yet, and yet, for generations every Javelin had been born of a good mother, and had had for his wife, a good woman. These things must count even in science. He had read the records in the Javelin book and noted how the force and energy of the earlier generations had sought expression in every kind of crime. Later, actual crimes disappeared from the pages and evil thoughts took their place. Malevolence ruled and tortured through two centuries and a half. Then, it seemed as if the power to do had waned. The desire was there, but the performing power was missing. The two last scions of the house had proved themselves as incapable of crime as they were incapable of noble effort. The force and energy of the race was spent utterly and the present man could be neither bad nor good, if he would.

Was it probable or possible that the first man

was right, when he had carved over his tomb, *Ecce homo qui non posuit Deum adjutorem suum?* Was this the answer to the riddle?

Nothing but an earthquake, or a mental shock equal to the full force of an earthquake, would ever bring Sir Christopher from death to life.

Then Lady Javelin spoke: "If anything happened to me, or—or to the children, would that do, you think?" Ready she was to sacrifice herself at a word, if it would avail.

But he answered, "No, not in the way I think you mean. Nothing to do with death, or sorrow, in which he has indulged himself *ad nauseam*. Something that would rouse a natural instinct to life would have the best chance—perhaps a supreme gladness, perhaps a fierce anger, anything which has sufficient life in it to carry him even temporarily out of himself."

Alas! Nothing on God's earth angered him. Nothing made him glad, for years and years and years, till a certain day when he saw his daughter as a woman grown—Miss Javelin.

PART III

"The Essence of the world is the invisible harmony in which all differences and oppositions are solved."—*Dr. H. Windelband.*

CHAPTER XX

MISS JAVELIN

"MISS JAVELIN by her mother, Lady Javelin." For a hundred years no such announcement had appeared in the list of those presented at court. There had been no Miss Javelin to present.

The above was seen in the morning papers by Miss Javelin's father. It arrested his attention. He turned from paper to paper till he found a full description of their gowns. No parental pride gleamed in his eyes as he read, merely a species of dull satisfaction. He went for a walk, and when he came back late in the afternoon, he hovered near the hall door, and was standing there waiting to greet them.

As they drove up and saw him, Lady Javelin felt a grip in the throat. Was the supreme gladness close at hand? Was he going to kiss his daughter? Fair and sweet and dainty, the girl stepped out of the carriage. "Father," she said and gave him her hand. He took it regarding her curiously. They all three went into the library and he stood there while they talked. But he was not listening, and there was still no pride in his gaze, only a puzzled curiosity.

When they went upstairs to dress for dinner, the girl linked her arm through the elder woman's.

"Mother dear, I think father was pleased to see us!"

She put on her court gown that night and after dinner she was further arrayed in her train and feathers for her grannie to see.

They were all sitting in the hall having their coffee when she came down the big staircase, the tulle lappets floating like a veil behind her; with the nodding plumes, she looked like a bride or a queen.

Lady J. put down her cup and held up her

lorgnettes—"Oh, my darling!" she said, "How beautiful you are! How beautiful!"

Crystal said nothing. She was watching her husband.

He rose from his chair suddenly as if moved by impulse, walked quickly towards the shining figure of his daughter, and stood watching her descend. She came down slowly to the last step but one, when she paused, her eyes then being on a level with his. He was gazing at her intently, looking at her as he had never looked at her before.

The two mothers held their breaths. They heard him say, "May I kiss you?" Then the girl's face was hidden by the man's for a moment.

"Father, do you like me?" she said with a little gay laugh, and swept on down the hall, holding him by the hand.

Neither Lady J. nor Lady Javelin moved The two figures reached them, and as the girl curtsied before her grandmother, Sir Christopher stood stiffly in front of his wife.

"I should like to have another daughter——"

Almost before the white satin figure rose again to her full height, he was gone. They heard him shut the door of his den.

The tragedy of it, that such a speech could not be met with a laugh.

No one spoke for a full minute. Three coffee cups were taken up and played with. The tension in the atmosphere was relieved by the simple dropping of a spoon. Then:

"I hope Mother darling, I can trust you not to give father another daughter. It would be most disconcerting." Think of the boys' feelings."

She gathered up her train with grace and said she would go to bed. She did not seem to be employing tact. She did better than that. She appeared unconscious that tact was needed, that all was not perfectly natural, and vanished.

The two women left in the hall looked at each other with smiles of unutterable sadness. There was every sort of emotion struggling

for supremacy: hope, fear, pleasure, thankfulness, regret.

"Thank God, Crystal! Thank God!"

"Yes."

"It was wonderful, my dear. He was
nearer himself than we have seen him for
years."

"Yes, for years."

They sat on talking till a late hour, softly,
quietly, hopeful fear warring with fearful
hope.

Before going to her own room, Lady Javelin
went to say good-night to Delicia. It was
dark in the room, but she felt her way to the
bed and two hands pulled her down on to it.

"Did I do right? Mother darling, was it
all right? We never thought, did we? It's
always like that. Something you're prepared
for never happens, and then when you've
forgotten about it, pop-bang you have to
decide in a minute."

"It was perfect!"

"Mother!" and a squeeze in the dark, "I
suppose there's something of the despot in

even the mildest, I mean the best of men. I thought it sounded so like a Turk when father said in that autocratic way, 'I should like to have another daughter.' Of course, he might have said 'I should like to have another wife'!"

"I should like to have another daughter," he was saying it down in his den.

"I should like to have another daughter," his wife was repeating it up in her room.

"I should like to have another daughter," Lady J. echoed it on her way home. Ah! how often she had said something similar in other years! Had her husband cared? Had her son cared whether his wife had gained her heart's desire? Had he cared then when they both were young? And now when, comparatively speaking, they both were old, when the children were grown up, when the fierce rebellion of nature against unsatisfied longings had long been patted to sleep by the woman, now when, if not impossible, it would at least be inconsiderate and inconvenient for the children's sake, he, the man, wanted what he might easily have had in the proper times and seasons. He wanted now what his wife had wanted always and had had to learn to do without.

In the small hours of the morning Lady J. tried to reach the plane of peaceful acquiescence wherein she had lived so long. She tried to see things as the Javelins had always seen them. She looked at the shape of the world as it appeared to Christopher. She recognised the failure and disappointment he must have encountered both in it and in himself, and she listened again to his speech of the night before and heard in it the almost stifled voice of Nature calling for help.

For years he had never come so near his wife as he had come last night when Delicia held him by the hand.

When Delicia held him by the hand, when Delicia held him—a long train of thought seemed born from these words. "A little child shall lead them," thrust itself in and was obviously rejected. Delicia was not a

16

little child. She was a full grown woman. Yet she, perhaps, could do for the man what his wife could not do, his mother could not do. Yes, perhaps Delicia could do it. Every Javelin all down the line had had a good mother, had also had a good wife. No record had ever mentioned a daughter. For a hundred years there had been no daughter. Delicia was the first in a hundred years.

It was just while Delicia touched him, that Sir Christopher had changed. While Delicia held his hand, he came near to being his former self. Was it possible that saving power might be in Delicia?

One woman could deaden a man. Poor Milly! it seemed the height of flattery to attribute anything so consequential to her, but it would require three women to make him alive. Three women, mother, wife, and daughter—a threefold relationship that no other Javelin had had for a hundred years. It could not be an accident. It could not be for nothing that, at Delicia's touch, the devil had gone out of the man, that Sir Christopher had come to

himself, when Delicia held him by the hand.
All the turbulent thoughts, both for herself
and her daughter-in-law, calmed down gently
and gradually.

Lady J. cherished the remembrance that
her son had come closer to his wife that evening than he had come for years. And if nearer
his wife, then nearer his mother, perchance
nearer to God. It was only momentary, and
no matter the reason, how or why. He had
just come, and his coming was a sign of
returning life. It might be the beginning of
the supreme gladness. A mistake now would
be fatal, and so easy to make. As the dawn
was breaking, she urged God on her knees
not to let Crystal make it.

In the days that followed, such fervency
seemed to have been imprudent. No oppor-
tunity for an error of judgment in delicate
matters was offered to Lady Javelin.

The shape of the world had been trans-
formed in a night for Sir Christopher by his
daughter Delicia. She was a full-blooded

young woman and she ousted memories of the anæmic Milly by one touch of her warm, firm hand.

Essays and articles of a flat defiance were left unfinished on his table while the father walked and rode and talked and listened with his daughter Delicia.

The world was round. Delicia said so. A spell was broken—Milly was dead, Delicia was very much alive. Delicia was the only living fact that mattered. He never misunderstood Delicia. He loved her.

It was pathetic to see him trying to please her—not that she was a hard task-mistress, but the soul of the man had to come so far when she called, as she did call imperiously many times a day. It had sunk so deep and so long in self that it was always in danger of getting away and hiding from those vigilant eyes waiting for it to respond to a thousand schemes.

All went well in the eyes of the two mothers, whose kind hearts, with the impersonal goodness of motherhood, brooded over the turn

of events. All went well for a week and a day.
Then the house filled up with young people.
The brothers returned for their vacations
and the cup of Delicia's joy was full.

They kissed her carelessly; brother-like they
teased her wickedly; they adored her spas-
modically; and from the evening of the day
in which the family were once more united,
Sir Christopher retreated into his den.

It was in vain they tried to keep him with
them, in vain they tried to prevent his leaving
them. Even Delicia following him to his door
was rebuffed sharply.

She wept. The poor child went to her
mother crying. After the uplifting experience of a week the sudden bump back to earth
shook her confidence in herself.

It had been so lovely, so ennobling to
succeed where others had failed; and now, to
have a door slammed in her pretty face, so
miserably ignoble. The tears had to fall.
What could the mother say to comfort—she
who had refused to give a like experiment a
chance?

Thus early in life, and at the hand of one inspired to love her, did Delicia learn that for every little step up, there is always a big step down.

The tears were dried. There were theatricals on hand. A very important part was assigned to Miss Javelin. She studied it with grace and rehearsed it with ease. The young lordling, her lover, threw himself at her feet, literally and metaphorically. The brothers, misunderstanding such old-time fashions, flew to rescue a sister from a situation full of fascination and peril, with the usual result. Ridicule defeated the brothers, who were thereafter applauded whenever they appeared.

With romance and excitement like this at its height, there was no time to think of papa sulking in his den. No, but there came a day when the young lover, privately rehearsing his part at the hall, with rather more fervour than when the whole cast was there, suddenly saw a giant figure loom in the doorway with eyes that flashed hatred and murder.

The arm that was round Delicia's waist

slipped inert away, the proper words stuck in the lover's throat, the temporary prompter prompted in vain, and then murmured things that were not in the book. The giant strode into the room and the furniture seemed to make gaps for his feet. Delicia slipped to the wall, gripping the chimney-piece, the lover stood firm, and the giant came on with fingers clawing the air.

One arm was suddenly raised as if to strike. Then the lover swerved, throwing himself between the giant and Delicia. The giant hitting out at that moment with all his force and hitting only the air, fell forward, with the whole weight of his body, crash, bang, crash, against the marble chimney-piece and on to the floor amongst the fire-irons and fender. Something shivered to bits.

CHAPTER XXI

THE OLD NURSERIES ARE USED AGAIN

"THE quietest room in the house, the very quietest, my dear lady, with another room adjoining for the nurse."

The village doctor, another doctor from London, and Billy's friend, were standing round Lady Javelin, a serious gravity having them all in possession.

"Can you think, or would you allow me to go and see?" Billy's friend detached himself from the group and moved towards the door. Lady Javelin bent her head, thinking.

"The old nurseries," she murmured and looked after him. "Wait for me," she called and went out quickly down the long passage and through double baize doors. Together they visited the disused rooms, in which a few dust sheets reigned along with silence.

The carpetless floors, spotlessly clean, the curtainless windows, open to the sun, the white tiled bathroom adjoining—all presented themselves to Billy's friend in the form of an invitation. A few hours' hard work would show a model hospital ward.

And here Sir Christopher was carried and lay, so the experts said, between life and death. His wife, who was not an expert, was sure he was nearer to Life. Womanlike she gave no reason. She merely knew.

After the operation was over, there followed a time of deep anxiety. The brain had suffered loss, and the whole system had received the sort of shock from which many a younger man had not recovered.

The house was empty of every one, even the children. The boys returned to their duties and Delicia, sorely against her will, went to the dower house across the park.

She prayed to stay with her mother, but Lady Javelin refused. Grannie was in need of comfort. Would not Delicia comfort her?

And to her mother-in-law she said, "Delicia is too young to be here alone, for I shall be with him all the time. May Delicia come to you?"

So that was the end for Delicia of her court gown, and her feathers, and her lordly lover, and her season in town, and her great success as her father's child. At least it seemed to be the end, at eighteen, but who knows?

The rest of the big house was desolate. Crystal, in a blue linen gown, lived entirely in the nursery wing, visited by the doctor, the agent, and the Rector.

She got through an immense amount of writing. She saw a new book through the press. She was busy from morning to night and she walked every day without fail to see the others across the park.

And Sir Christopher lay in his bed, alive but knowing nothing, and the waiting time seemed very, very long to all but Lady Javelin and Billy's friend. Matters of life and

death cannot be hastened, especially life
if it is to be strong and vigorous when it
comes.

"Though the mills of God grind slowly,"
said Billy's friend, a dear thing but not given
to originality of thought, "yet they grind
exceeding small."

And Lady Javelin had said, "Yes, but all my
life I have been one of those inclined to give
an extra turn to the mill handle when I have
seen a chance."

"With the danger of passing uncrushed
grain——"

"Yes, one finds that out afterwards."

And the figure lying on the bed, unconscious of the outward life going on around
him, was dimly conscious of a vagueness and a
vapour through which something that seemed
to be himself was trying to push. It was all so
vague, all such a cloud, that effort was useless;
besides there was not enough ego in a mist to
make an effort to be free of the mist.

This went on for æons of time. The body
slept and ate and was cared for without making

any impression on the mind. For those who cared, it was like caring for the dead.

Then one day, the vagueness broke and the soul of Sir Christopher stirred. The next day it opened its eyes, or it may have been the next week or the next month—the soul had no account with Time. It just opened its eyes and saw the light. It was very distressing, and the soul tried to shut them again. The light showed so many things it did not want to see. After that a fight began, a very unequal fight. Darkness against light, and the darkness did all in its power to reign supreme, but the strength of the light was such that the darkness was soon reduced to a shadow dependent for its very existence on keeping the other side of the light.

And after what seemed to be ages of a cotton-wool sort of conflict, in which no sounds were heard, the eyes of the soul seemed to connect with the eyes of the mind and to look through the eyes of the body.

And the first thing on which Sir Christopher looked with dawning intelligence was a sunny room with a fire and a woman. He shut out the vision, shutting his bodily eyes in order that he might look within.

A woman of that kind awoke some familiar memory, which it would take him years to trace. With eyes always shut, he began.

A blue and white figure bending over a fire, and round the fire a high wire guard—that was enough to puzzle over at first. Then the far away sounds that had been muffled so long became suddenly clear. He recognised them as voices,—quiet, soft voices that spoke as if he were asleep. He hoped they would not find out he was awake. He must work out the situation by himself and discover who and what he was.

He heard the voices, but he did not understand a word of what they said. He did not want to. He was so tired, he wanted to stay in the cloud or the mist where details and outlines were blurred.

Then a door opened somewhere in the cloud and he was conscious of a movement beside him. A voice spoke and he knew it. He had heard it before. The voice seemed to touch his forehead in a peculiar manner and the touch opened his eyes. They remained open in a wide, fixed stare.

Two people were close to him. One was the blue and white nurse. He wondered how he knew and had always known she was a nurse. The other, in black, was his mother.

A confusion of sounds followed, and he got away into the grey mist again as quick as he could. It was an awful revelation that had come to him, an awful revelation. He knew himself now for what he was. He was a new-born baby.

From that moment the quietness went out of his life. All was confusion without and within. He was seldom, if ever, able to get away into the grey cloud. People, always people, were coming to look at him. He would not look at them, but he was able to distinguish sounds and even voices from one another. There was one he knew well because it always said the same thing. It always said:

"I wish he would open his eyes and look at you."

Not he. He knew better than that with the friendly, grey mist receding from him farther and farther every day.

So he fed and slept and wondered and listened.

Everything confirmed him in his idea that he was really a new-born thing, just come into the world, and gradually he began to be rather interested in the processes of keeping him alive. He still kept his outward eyes shut as much as possible and gained his knowledge chiefly from within, hoping thereby to deceive "the people" whose presence drove away the grey cloud.

"I think he's beginning to take notice. Of course he's been conscious now for some time." This in a gruff voice, while another voice, deeper and more disturbing, said something in reply.

"Well, young man, let us have a look at you."

The Christopher lying on the bed could not

believe this remark was intended for him.
It was a queer way to speak to a baby, unless
of course it was the baby's father. It must be
his father.

He had no curiosity to see him, not even
when the gruff voice said, "Don't hurry him,
don't hurry him, give him all the time he
wants! He's making very good progress."
Then the voice was lost in more sound.

Another time he heard the same voice say,
"We've made a splendid job of this, Nurse,
a wonderful job."

And one of the women in blue said, "I'm
glad you're satisfied, sir. It's been a long
case." Then he fell off asleep.

When he woke, he opened his outward eyes
quite inadvertently, and they fell on the
woman sitting at a table writing. He had
seen her before. She was the first woman he
had seen after he was born. She never worried
him. She just sat there, and he lay and looked
at her.

After a bit he began to wonder about her.
He wished she would move. Next he moved

himself, very successfully. It made her look up. He saw her eyes across the room.

She came near to him and bent down.

"Do you know me, darling?" Then, after a pause, "Don't try. Shut your eyes again, and go to sleep." Just the way a woman speaks to a baby.

He was getting very knowing now. He was beginning to understand that he generally had to do as he was told, and because this woman told him to go to sleep, he wanted to keep awake and see why she wanted him to go to sleep.

He shut his eyes, and she went back to her writing. He heard the little soothing sound of the pen on the paper; then he looked again to see if it were safe. It was quite safe. She was very busy, and he watched her for times and times and times.

Then one day he had a desire to hear his own voice. He said, "Mother," when several people were in the room. The one he knew long ago to be his mother disengaged herself from the rest and came and took his hand.

17

"Yes, my son," followed by great confusion again, and a long silence.

He knew a lot of things now. He knew himself to be a silly, helpless baby. He knew his father from the doctor, and he knew his mother from the nurse, and he knew the woman who never worried. He must be getting very old.

After a bit he took his own situation and every one round it for granted. The only one he puzzled over was the writing woman. Who was she? What was she always doing in his room, and why?

There came to be a time when she was there alone. His nurse went away and nobody else, not even his father, or the doctor, or his mother ever came to disturb his dreams. This happened every day. He formed a plan in secret.

He had been so successful with "Mother," he would try the others. He said, "Nurse," one day, and the nurse came at his call, and no confusion followed. He said, "Father," when he heard the gruff voice beside him, and met only silence.

"Father," but no, he was wrong somewhere. Nurse said, "That's the first mistake he's made," and the gruff voice answered, "No matter, what can I do for you, my boy?"

But he was bored by them with his failure and shut his inward and outward eyes.

He did not try speaking for some time, he waited to be sure. But as the days passed and he grew familiar with the room—the sounds without, the people and the scenes within—his spirit grew restive. It was being kept in bondage, in the bondage of ignorance. He must know more about himself, about the writing woman.

He and she were alone again. It was the time when nobody came. He wanted to attract her attention and talk to her. If he said nurse or mother, she would not know how sensible he was, and he did not know how to call her. He thought, and as he thought, he wanted her to speak to him so much that, when she would not look up and see, he began to cry, just like a baby.

The writing woman stopped, and came over

to him. She took her handkerchief and wiped
his eyes.   It smelt so good he thought he
would cry again later. Then she went down
on the floor beside him and put her face quite
close to his.

"What is it, dear?"

"Where am I?"

"In the nursery, your own, old nursery at
home."   That confirmed theory number one
about himself.

The woman on the floor waited.

Then, "How old am I now?"

"You 're forty-eight now; going to be
forty-nine next birthday. I am the same."

He shrank from her. She was telling a lie.
It was not fair to tell lies to children.

She seemed to know there was something
wrong, for she smiled at him and said, "Do
you know who I am?"

He shook his head.

"Never mind. It does n't matter. We can
wait for that."

"Does matter! Want to know! Tell me!"

"I 'm Crystal."

He only looked blank.

The voice seemed to hesitate. "I'm Crystal, your wife."

He gazed at her fixedly. Then his eyes began to smile.

"Got a wife?"

She nodded.

"I thought I was a baby!"

She bent nearer him caressingly. "So you are, the biggest baby a woman ever had to deal with, but you're also my husband, if you don't mind."

"But I thought I was a baby, just born."

His mouth twitched at the corners and he laughed faintly, weakly. The woman on her knees laughed with him. The tension of years seemed to snap suddenly.

Some one opened the door behind them, paused in amazement, and shut it again. The man on the bed whispered, "Don't go— Just born——"

And the woman couldn't be grave, not if she tried.

CHAPTER XXII

DELICIA CHAPERONES HER GRANDMOTHER

" DARLING Mother,
    " Now that father 's better, can you
spare an hour to your poor little daughter?
She does want to see you.   There 's something she has wished to talk about for ages,
but she could not bother you.   Will you come
to tea?   Grannie is longing to sit with father!
                    " Your loving,
                              " DELICIA."

Lady Javelin read the note at breakfast
and for reply sent to ask her mother-in-law if
she would like to come late in the afternoon
and spend an hour with the invalid.

The two mothers met half-way across the
park and sat on the seat under the beech tree.
They smiled as they talked, and both looked

as if a kind hand had smoothed their faces in the last few days. They parted with a nod and a laugh.

Delicia was waiting in the garden and linked her arm in her mother's.

"I 've ordered tea out here. I think you 've been indoors too much."

Lady Javelin said Ha! but she enjoyed having the child take care of her.

" Well, what do you want to talk to me about? I suppose I can guess."

"I don't think so, but wait till they 've finished bringing tea. The kettle 's got to come."

"Very well. Your father had another excellent night. He 's doing better than, I believe, they ever expected."

"So glad, Mother dear, but of course we knew that early this morning. Now, it 's quite safe. I want to talk to you about Grannie."

"About Grannie! What 's the matter with her?"

"Well, I don't think there 's anything the

matter, but I think I 'd like there to be. Can
you guess?"

"For goodness' sake, what do you mean?"

"You know Sir Guy Larkin?"

"Yes."

"Well, can't you guess now?"

"Not in the least. He 's old enough to be
your great grandfather."

"Grandfather will do."

"Delicia, what can you be thinking of?"

"Why just that, Mother. He adores
Grannie. I know he does. I don't mean he
has said so to me, but I can see it, anybody
can see it—except Grannie. I don't think it
occurs to her. Why shouldn't they marry?"

"Marry! My dear child, you take my
breath away. Lady Larkin has only been
dead——"

"Years, my dear Mother."

"It may be a year or two."

"And it 's so dull for them both! Each in a
big house all alone, and loving each other all
the time."

"Delicia!"

"They do, I know they do."

"You little matchmaker! What made you think of such a thing?"

"It just seems most natural and they are n't either of them old really."

"Only seventy, I think!"

"That 's in years. I mean in themselves. They are quite young still."

"Grannie is nineteen years older than your father. He is forty-eight. So that makes her sixty-seven. Sir Guy is probably older, about seventy as I said."

"Well, you won't object, you and father, if I encourage it, will you?"

"You encourage it! No. We 've no right to object but——"

"But what, Mother."

"I think, Delicia, it 's a risk seldom worth running. 'To gain a lover and lose a friend.'"

"I don't think it would be so in this case. I believe it would be a splendid combination affair."

"My dear child, how long has this been in your mind?"

"Almost ever since I came to stay. You see, Sir Guy was awfully upset about father and he used to come here every day to enquire, and he and Grannie had long talks, and sometimes he used to walk up to the house with me to find out the latest news, and he always talked about Grannie, either as she is now or as she used to be when Grandpapa was alive. I 've heard lots of things about the family from him. I don't think we 're much to boast of, do you? Javelin 's a very old name, of course, and that counts for something now-a-days, but Grandpapa seems to have been odd and the rest bad. Anyway Sir Guy is an old dear. I simply love him, and should like to have him as a relation of some sort, and Grandpapa seems the most suitable. He simply adores Grannie. What can we do to help?"

"Nothing! No, Delicia, I am quite firm about that. I won't hinder, but equally I will not help. It 's too dangerous. True friendship between a man and a woman is so rare and beautiful, marriage, my dear, might spoil it."

"You 're talking now just like your Wilhelmina, where she says 'the finest love is unadulterated by pity or contempt.'"

"I thought I said you were not to read my manuscripts."

"I did n't read it, darling. I happened to pass it lying open just at that page, and saw it without reading it—you know how one does."

"No, Delicia, you 're very beguiling, but it won't do. I think now father 's better that perhaps you 'd best come home. Only I 'm with him so much——"

"And poor Grannie 's so lonely if she is n't to marry Sir Guy——"

"Nonsense! I must see about it. I 'll talk to your father."

"Does he ever say he wants me back? Does he remember about that awful night?"

Lady Javelin shook her head.

"Never? Does n't he know what happened?"

"We think not. He has gone quite back to years ago, when you were all tiny, almost before you were born, but of course he may remember any day."

"Does n't he know he broke his head? Does n't he know some of his brains——"

"No, darling, and I hope he never will. All is going on well. He is really better in every way."

"Perhaps they were packed too tight before, and now there is more room for them to work easily!"

"Perhaps."

"If he does n't remember my existence, I can't come home—not to be of any use, I mean. How could you explain my official position in his room? Me so young and so fair! I had better stay here and chaperone Grannie."

CHAPTER XXIII

THE WIND BLOWETH WHERE IT LISTETH

A GLORIOUS Sunday, the tenth day of June. All the family had gone to church, leaving Sir Christopher sitting by open windows where, when the bells stopped ringing, he could hear the organ and the chanting of the choir, even the voice of the Rector through the wide west door.

He had books beside him, but he did not read. He lay back in his chair gazing out into the garden, listening to the hum of the insects mingling with the hum of the human congregation.

He was quite alone, wide awake, and fully conscious. Yet he heard the sound of laughter. Soft at first, it increased in volume and had a derisive note in it that jarred the quietness of the day.

The laughter came out of the air and drowned the organ and the voices of prayer and praise. It shrieked in his ears with fiendish glee. Words were said, but he could not distinguish them from the demoniacal screams, as devoid of mirth as they were full of venom.

Presently he recognised himself as the centre of this ridiculous tintinnabulation. He, Sir Christopher Javelin, was being laughed to scorn, but by whom, and why?

Something familiar caught his ear out of the hubbub, and he listened intently, trying to piece together the past and the present. The laughter bubbled and died and the voices became clear and distinct, rising with quiet strength above the hideous din,

"*Ecce homo qui non posuit Deum adjutorem suum.*"

"*Ecce homo, Ecce homo—*" and more laughter, gradually fading away into a long silence. The man lay back in his chair, his outward eyes fixed on the inward vision; his outward ears hearing an inward song.

He saw people, always people again, walk-

ing in a grey mist. He felt the cloud, the old
friendly cloud, wrap him round with familiar
touch and then—nothing.

The Javelin family and retinue came out of
church. They stood talking with enquiring
neighbours and sympathetic friends, then
they wandered desultory-fashion round the
gardens, round the stables, out of the kennels,
the same round that every Javelin had made
for hundreds of years. A gong rang and they
came trooping over the lawn.

"Heavenly day, Father, isn't it? Are you
enjoying it?"

He said "Yes," because it was obvious
they noticed nothing wrong.

His wife came and stood beside him, pulling
off her gloves. Something in her eyes made
him feel she saw a change.

He said abruptly. "Wasn't there rather a
row in church this morning? I heard some
very discordant sounds."

"No, they sang very well."

"Who preached?"

"The Rector."

"What about?"

Lady Javelin gave a final tug and freed her hand of the long grey glove. "It was about being born again!—" she smiled at him as if they had an understanding.

He put out his hand and pulled the end of the glove pulling her hand with it.

"What was the text?" As she hesitated, he laughed, "You've forgotten it already!"

"No, but it was rather a long one, about the wind blowing where it listeth."

'Yes?"

"And thou hearest the sound thereof, but canst not tell whence it cometh or whither it goeth, so is every one that is born of the spirit."

He nodded, kissed the hand he held, and said, "I would like to see the Rector this afternoon. Will you tell him?"

The two men sat together in the same room later in the day, and the elder of the two listened to the curious experience of the younger. His was a sympathetic nature and he fully believed such an experience was possible.

They had that morning in church chanted the psalm in English, the Latin version of which had been heard by Sir Christopher. How or why he could not explain, but the sense of the words had been so long connected with the Javelin family that doubtless they would easily reach a member of the family with the original sound in which they had first been heard.

Sir Christopher asked for the context, and when it was given to him, he was amazed. He repeated the words over to himself, "and shall laugh him to scorn." "Yes, my dear sir, they did that, but it was not the righteous. At least, I cannot believe that those hideous sounds came from the minds of the righteous, or else I have different ideas of what it must be to be righteous. Still, I was laughed to scorn this morning. No doubt about that. Laughed to scorn I was, and you all in church shouting the reason, 'Lo, this is the man.' Well, you 've known me man, and boy, for forty

18

years, and you 've known me always as the man that took not God for his strength. Now I want you to understand that from henceforth I intend to do so."

The Rector leaned forward to catch the scarcely audible words. He responded in a whisper, "Amen," "Amen," twice over and very gravely.

CHAPTER XXIV

SIR CHRISTOPHER TRIES TO PAY HIS DEBTS

"Once to every Man and Nation
Comes the moment to decide."

THE moment had come to Sir Christopher Javelin and he had made his decision.

After that life bore a wholly different aspect from what it did before. It was as though he had hitherto lived with a crape veil over his face, and now it had suddenly lifted. That was the difference.

Yet, though he had come out of a gloomy past, it had not been black with crime like that of some of his ancestors. He had not led an evil life, merely an inadequate one. He had, when he came to analyse the last twenty years in the light of the last few weeks, he knew he had led a miserably dull existence, totally unenlivened by passionate joys, passionate sorrows, or even the average pleasures to be gained from his position. It had all been on a dead level of—he tried to find another word. Only one was suitable, and he knew it, yet he did not want to use it. All a dead level of—he must own it, with the fresh light pouring in and illuminating the dark places of his mind: his life had been a dead level of mediocrity.

Mediocrity! He had not been a bad son, as sons go, but he had missed being a particularly good one. He had not been a bad husband in the sense of deserting his wife openly, but then he had not been the best. He had not been a bad father; he had never illtreated his children; but he had not been a good one. He had not been a bad neighbour. He had never introduced undesirables to those amongst whom he lived; but he had not added to the gaiety of nations in any way, not even in his own little plot of ground. He had not propagated lies when he had written on the shape of the world. He had published what he honestly believed. It was a stupid belief. He saw that, now the veil was off his face, and though he need not be actually ashamed of his literary output, he could not be proud, as he would like to be.

He had not made bad friendships, not bad ones, but in the last twenty years he knew he had not made a good one, and he had done nothing to keep those good ones already made.

That any of them were still his, was due to no effort on his part—that he was well aware. His mother's friendship? Was that his because he was so worthy of it? His wife's friendship? Was that retained because he was so lovable? His children's, because he was such a perfect companion? His neighbours' and friends', because he had always loved them as himself?

And then Milly? There was only one answer he could give when he thought of the shape of the world as he had seen it with Milly. He groaned inwardly as he gave it.

A phrase he had read some time in a morning paper occurred to his mind as unpleasantly apt to Sir Christopher Javelin. It rose up in his memory something like this:

"And no sense of the ridiculous, no perception of the awful way he cheapened himself when he bellowed his homage to mediocrity, ever entered his Philistine head."

He had bellowed his homage for twenty years, not to the Most High but to mediocrity.

When a man or a woman receives a blow, struck at the heart through pride or vanity, their manner of enduring the pain or agony resulting therefrom, proves to a great degree their character as a human being. Do they fall to earth and lie there writhing worm-like, miserable objects to all beholders? Do they hit back, blow for blow, suggesting thereby the elementary forces of primitive nature? Do they crawl out of sight, brave but silent, hiding their hurts and themselves thenceforth from the eyes of the world? Do they rise up savage with pain, crippled and maimed, yet declaring themselves untouched even while blood drips from the wound? Do they, after the first stunning effect is over, do they acknowledge the wisdom and strength of the blow, submit to the remedies offered, often of peace and quiet, and do they emerge therefrom better equipped for the future?

When Sir Christopher "came to himself," he knew that the least he could do was to make the *Amende honorable*, not only for negative neglect but for positive perversity. He must try and make up to others for what they had suffered because of him.

He thought of his mother, requiring a prop and stay in her declining years. He would offer himself. He would ask her to use him as a son who could be relied on. He would prove to her that all the old affection between them existed still. It had gone to sleep for a time, it was true, but now, now the veil was off his face, he was awake.

Then his children. He owed them years of time and devotion. The boys were away. He would begin with Delicia. He would make the rest of her life as happy for her as he had made that week, that blissful week which had brought him so near to death that the result had been Life. Yes, he owed Delicia a good deal. He would repay her, repay her, no matter what it cost.

There was Crystal. He must think what he could do for Crystal. It would take a lot of thinking. He could begin at once with some of the others.

So he began, but he found he was too late. Too late for his mother. Her old friend, Sir Guy Larkin, left nothing undone that ought to be done to ensure her comfort and prosperity in her declining years. He even offered her love that had been tried in the fire and that would not fail. Sir Christopher found they had no place for him, more than the place he had chosen for himself, in the last twenty years. That, and no more, was still his.

Too late with his mother, he turned with bright hopes to his daughter. There at least he would be in time. He began but something was amiss. He could not recapture the spirit of that blissful week. He was too late, and indirectly she told him so. Prettily and sweetly she asked him to let her go.

He had vowed to repay Delicia all that he owed her. He had thought to do this in his own coin. But to Delicia it was worthless. She thanked him for all his good intentions towards her. She spoke charmingly of the little time when she had been his companion, and now that he was no longer quite blind, quite deaf, and unutterably stupid, he understood without any words how he might have enjoyed a daughter's companionship for twenty years, had he not been "bellowing his homage" elsewhere.

And now in order to repay Delicia for the saving grace which had come to him through her, he must let her go. She no longer wanted him. She wanted the man who had come between them on the day the old self-absorbed Christopher Javelin fell at his daughter's feet and died in a fit of jealous rage, the day the new Sir Christopher was born.

He asked her for time to pay this debt. He must count the cost; he must fight it out. If he paid, he must pay gladly, willingly, to satisfy Delicia. He knew that. No grudging

fulfilment of the letter or the law would please
the child who had unconsciously taught him
the value of the spirit.

If he did not give his consent, she would
never marry the man she loved. She felt they
both owed it to him, her father, to remain
unmarried if he chose that it should be so.
Therefore, to repay Delicia in full, Sir Christopher must not only let his daughter go, but
he must teach himself to be glad to give her
to the very man whose once momentary near-
ness to her had roused in him that frenzy of
rage and fear.

"He will never do it," his mother said;
"you can hardly expect it of him. No Javelin
forgets or forgives."

"No other Javelin," Crystal said "*mais
nous avons changé tout cela.*"

"Perhaps, but as a bit of worldly advice
merely, I think Delicia had better have
another string to her bow."

"No thank you, Grannie. I too am a
Javelin and I have given my word."

As a preliminary step Sir Christopher sent

for the lordly young lover whose play had been spoilt such a long time ago. Circumstances naturally made conversation between the two men somewhat difficult, but the difficulties vanished strangely soon, because they were mutually felt to be an obstacle to Delicia's happiness.

Thus in a comparatively short space of time, and in a manner well worth the waiting, did Delicia gain the desire of her heart. She saw "every little root of bitterness" gradually disappear. She saw the crooked made straight and the rough places plain. She saw even the desert rejoice and blossom as a rose, when she saw her father become a friend of the man who had chosen her for his wife. Her own love and gratitude overflowed from the one to the other till each at his best responded blithely to the best in each.

Dear Delicia! The Millennium seemed at hand.

CHAPTER XXV

SIR CHRISTOPHER LEARNS WHY MATRIMONY WAS ORDAINED

BUT the hardest and steepest bit of the way had yet to be climbed. Sir Christopher found, as many have found, that though we can all go out of Eden, of our own free wills, at any time we choose, it 's devilish difficult to get back again with the flaming sword of our own pride always guarding the way.

And civilised man can hardly go out of a woman's life merely to please himself, and then expect to stroll back again when the fancy takes him, without the courtesy of first finding out whether his return would be pleasing to her; or if he does, such conduct savours too much of the animal world to be

284

worth a thought, from the woman, of anger or of regret.

One day, later on, they two being alone in the house, Crystal was busy writing as usual, when her husband opened the door, and there came a smell of burning. She lifted her head, her nostrils contracting. "What is it?" she said, "a chimney?"

"Only some papers of mine. I've been making a bonfire. You're busy, I see."

She laid her pen down on the table. "Not too busy, if you want me."

"How characteristic!"

"Of me, or of women in general?"

"Of both."

He walked to the window at the back of her table, looked out, turned round, leaning against the centre bar and facing her.

"Must you be always writing?"

"No."

"But it means a lot to you?"

"It has meant a good deal, but now there's not the same necessity."

Christopher looked at her as if he would

read a meaning into her words. Then, "I wish I knew why," he said, "but I have no right to ask."

"Indeed you have the right. I wrote, in the first place, because I wanted money to bring the extra water supply to the village. I went on writing, because I did not care to dress myself and the children entirely at your expense. I am writing now, because it's a habit, and I seem to have a superabundant amount of creative force in my system which must have a vent; also I have a scheme I should like to carry out."

"Crystal, did you ever want for money?"

"I wanted enough to make me independent, and so save you being worried by details, when you were busy." She smiled at him. "Did n't it ever occur to you that, with the children growing up and everything, I never asked you for money? How did you think I managed?"

"Then you circumvented me about the Stores. I meant you to get everything there. Then I should have paid."

"I know, the Stores are excellent for many

things, but in the matter of clothes—I just used my own discretion. You always liked Delicia's clothes, did n't you?"

"Always, and yours. May I have any bills that have not been paid?"

"Yes, with pleasure, if you wish."

"Another thing. What allowances are the boys having?"

"The same that you had in your father's lifetime divided between them, and I supplement the rest."

"They always tell you when they want money?"

"So far. They have been very good, not really extravagant."

"They know that you make it?"

"Yes, and are delightful about it."

"In what way?"

"Oh, they are—it sounds conceited—but they are proud and excited and interested. Besides, they really help me."

"Does any one else help you?"

"Any one? Why every one does in their different way."

"Except me."

"You, most of all."

The man shook his head.

"Most of all. If it had not been for you, I should never have written a word, just brought up children, and kept pigs and chickens, and messed about in the garden. It was you who taught me to write."

"As a stop-gap?"

"I wonder."

The man in the window put his hands in his pockets and snapped coins one against the other.

"I have been reading over the marriage service since Delicia's wedding. It's thoroughly practical, as well as mystical. I find I promised to endow you 'with all my worldly goods'—'All,' and it does not seem to me you have had half, or even a quarter—no don't interrupt. That you have not chosen to ask for it is extra goodness on your part. It in no way justifies my neglect. People who do not intend to keep these promises, should not make them. Then—the reasons for which matrimony is ordained. I only attended to the first as long as it suited me, I resented the second, and I forgot the third. What penance can you suggest as in any way adequate?"

The woman shook her head. "There are 'beams' in my eyes."

The man ignored the suggestion. "Must I find my own?"

"No."

"What then?"

"You have been doing penance for so many years. Do you think you need do any more?"

"But that was all involuntary. I must do one—willingly."

"Chris, you are beloved!"

"Something hard—for you."

He had done it, without knowing it. His wife showed him the ashes of his sacrifice still smouldering on the altar of their empty home. He had not offered that which had cost him nothing. He had let his daughter go when all that was human in him craved to keep her.

19

He had put her happiness before his own. He had done that with regard to her husband which no unregenerate soul could ever have done, and his wife had noted these things and kept them in her heart.

As they talked thus together, it seemed to her that the third reason for which matrimony was ordained was being amply fulfilled, and when she said so—Glory be to God—he understood!

CHAPTER XXVI

THE EARTH GRAVITATES TOWARDS THE SUN

A MAN in a far country looking through his English mail paused time after time scanning the various handwritings and postmarks. One letter he laid aside, and took up another, put that with the first one unopened, and started on a third. It was the Christmas mail from home and he evidently expected news. He seemed fastidious as to the quarter from which it should first reach him.

He got a large cigar and stretched himself in a deck chair, thoroughly comfortable and at ease. Then he began. At the end of an hour he was sitting upright, his long legs on either side of the chair, his half smoked cigar on the edge of the tray, and the letters and papers between his knees.

He had gone a long, long way. He was listening to the sound of wedding bells, and they seemed to ring for people of all ages.

He took up the letters again one by one. They all told the same tale, of a world that was romping round, whose motive power was Love.

To the man in the far country, the one that appealed to him most, personally, was Aunt Patricia's. It was full of love for him, with its mild regrets at Milly's death and its strong concern for his consequent loneliness, its fervent hopes of seeing him again with this rumour of a Home appointment and its beautiful references to the memory of an idealised Captain Fitz-James.

Yet he put it down quicker than most.

There was Aunt Judy's, full of the Woman's Movement—not the women of her family. They, she frankly owned, were past praying for. Every one of them had given herself over body and soul to the keeping of some man. She alone of them all stood out and worked single handed for the cause, which was gaining glory and recruits from day to day. Love of womanhood with Judy far transcended love of man or child. It seemed a lopsided love. There was one sentence in this letter that the man turned back and read through again.

"You will have heard of Christopher's remarkable recovery in every way, long before this. It always puzzles me that a husband of any sort can be such a priceless possession to a woman of brains. Don't trouble to answer this with an essay on grapes, sour or otherwise!"

Billy paused a long time over these few words. He gnawed his under lip at the corner, as if unconscious of what he was doing. An inward vision rose before him, to which he unhesitatingly added a note of interrogation, and then sat and looked at it.

There was a short letter from sweet Lady J., full of praise of her daughter-in-law, full of hope for the future, full of happiness for herself and others, and a long one from the

specialist friend, more than usually full of
interest.

"I have never been so keen over any case in
my whole life," he wrote, "as I have been over
the Javelin affair. Physically, morally, spiritually it has absorbed me and my younger
colleague utterly. I had diagnosed the physical side of the case correctly long ago when
I visited the father of the present man, and
later events have proved this to be so. Sir
Christopher's accident released the suspected
pressure on the brain and in the words of
Scripture made 'all things work together for
good.'

"As a medical man I can truly say I have
never had such splendid assistance from the
ladies of any family before. The actual
nursing done by Lady Javelin was very fine.
In reading their historical records, I have often
marvelled at the characteristics of those many
women, who, not Javelin born, were yet called
upon to endure, gladly if they could, all the
singular eccentricities of the race. They had
never failed through twelve generations, and

in the twelfth, as, I think, a result of this,
was born a daughter of the line, who, in
rousing to life a natural instinct, has unconsciously worked a miracle.

"I use the word advisedly; for morally, he
has a grip in life; spiritually, he is new-born.
Therefore, to see Sir Christopher as he is now,
is to see a miracle, and you, I am sure, would
agree with me. May I hope that before long
we shall have that pleasure together, as Lady
Javelin tells me you are 'wanted' over here in
high places. With them, I rejoice to know of
this, and beg to congratulate you with all my
heart."

The post so far was interesting, but two
letters still remained. The best till the
last!

Billy shut his eyes and shuffled the letters
round on the cane seat. There is something
of the child in most men. The letter he
opened ran thus:

"A happy Christmas to you, dear Billy,
from us both; and when are you coming

home? We all think you have been gone quite long enough and hope you will accept the offer which rumour says is to reach you immediately. We have been having some difficult days over here and life has been rather chequered for us all. Chris and I have been passing through the Renaissance. I cannot write about it. . . . He is extremely busy with a lot of public work—the same he used to do long ago, yet not too busy to attend the first night of my new play, which pleased him so much we stayed on in town for him to attend another evening performance and a matinée. *Que pensez-vous de cela, mon cher?* Now listen to this. I am going to give up play-writing for literature, prompted partly by ambition, partly by boredom with the colloquial style. I thought I was to be called on to lay down my fluent pen for always, because Chris seemed to have more writing to do than he could manage alone and liked me to help him. But after seeing the play, he would not hear of this, and instead, Billy, he offered to help me. I wish you could see us. In my thirst for fame I am seeking to use only Shakespeare's language, rejecting all words of modern Latin

derivation. Chris is an adept at spotting
these, when together we substitute the Anglo-
Saxon. My first book written in this style
may interest you. It is to be dedicated to
'An Exile for Chivalry,' unless I choose that
for the title. Which would you like best?
A. S. or Lat.?

"All the children are doing well: Delicia
blissful and the son-in-law, a dear; both boys
gay yet satisfactory, Chriskin growing like
you in many of his ways—ways which I have
no inclination to correct.

"*Àdieu*, with love from the entire family.

"Always your friend,

"CRYSTAL J."

As he read the last paragraph, his eyes
twinkled, and he laughed—a sort of re-
strained chuckle and pressed the paper to
his lips.

Still that light touch on the heavy reins of
circumstance, which Billy as a sportsman so
adored! Would any one reading this woman's
letter guess that she and tragedy had lived
together hand in hand, for years, and years,
and years?

Even as he read, he who knew it all, the triumphant spirit of her seemed to him to bubble over in every line and dare the tragedy to show its face. He adored her. He always had. He always would. Present or absent, it made no difference; but the mad violence of his adoration had been tempered, chastened. The lion was tamed. His claws, had they still needed cutting, were further cut by this, "Chris and I have been passing through the Renaissance." He could go home now. She would find him quite harmless, tame, possibly dull. Would she? Others might. He knew she never would.

He forgot there was another letter left unopened amongst the pile. He got up and walked about his garden. He ate his midday meal. He attended to business and later in the evening he found it.

The old Rector from home had written him a long account of all the doings of the last twelve months. It was a yearly letter that had never failed to reach the man in the far country. It gave him the news of his neigh-

bours high and low, rich and poor, sorry and
glad. It told him of weddings and funerals,
of births and marriages and deaths. It went
on with a vivid description of Sir Christopher's
accident, and what led up to it, and what
followed after. Then, in old-fashioned phrase-
ology, it pointed out how in the writer's own
mind he had seen his beloved Lady Javelin
have the desire of her heart spiritually granted
her. After many years, the nurseries at the
hall had been used again, and the Rector,
calling one afternoon and being told he could
go upstairs unannounced, had gone up, had
opened the door quietly, and had seen
Lady Javelin kneeling on the floor caress-
ing something and laughing softly beside
the bed.

"I knew then," he wrote, "that all was well.
I knew then she would remember no more the
pain of former years, for the old, old reason,
my dear sir, for joy that a man was born
into the world.

" Having lived to see this, I feel that my
days must be numbered, and I am ready to

sing my *Nunc Dimittis*. Yet I cannot help
thinking of my successor here and wondering.
Should he find it difficult in years to come to
choose fresh words in place of those so
continuously suitable in the dear family
records of the past, I hope it may occur
to him that, discarding the language of the
Old Testament, he may choose the Greek
of the New, and may perchance sign his
name below this expression of the great
fact which gives us all the spirit of hope
and joy":

"'Αγαπητοί, νῦν τέκνα θεοῦ ἐσμέν, καὶ οὔπω ἐφανερώθη τί
ἐσόμεθα."

The eyes that read so far grew misty to
outward things. The vivid inward vision
was all the man could see: a woman in her
nursery, kneeling on the floor, her arms round
something new-born. Was it body, was it
spirit? What did it matter? The woman was
laughing softly.

This was the shape of the world at its best—
at its very, very best.

"Out of mine eyes I strove the tears to keep.
　Out of my song I tore the note of pain.
　I wrote of sunshine 'mid the falling rain,
That none might read my words, and, reading,
　　weep—
And since it is ordained that man shall reap
　Naught but the harvest of his scattered grain,
　God grant I may in later years regain
Seed that was sown in furrows rough and deep.

"Oh, empty granaries! I fain would fill
　Each vacant storehouse full unto the brim!
　But even as I write, my eyes grow dim
For youth half spent and Time that stands
　　not still,
　Yet should I bring one sack—one sack—to Him,
His mercy would suffice for Deed and Will."

THE END